SAINTS, CROOKS & SLAVERS

History of a Bristol House and its People

PETER CULLIMORE

Including how to research past residents of your own house

BY SUE CULLIMORE

BRISTOL BOOKS

Bristol Books CIC, The Courtyard, Wraxall,
Wraxall Hill, Bristol, BS48 1NA

Saints, Crooks & Slavers,
written and researched by Peter Cullimore
With tips on house history research by Sue Cullimore

Published by Bristol Books 2020

ISBN: 9781909446243

Design: Joe Burt

CONTENTS

HISTORICAL TIMELINE

Dates	Owners/Occupants	Trades/Occupations	Significant Events
1776			Deeds refer to Order of Conveyance between J Crook and Wm Harrison.
Pre-1790s	**Edward Bearpacker** Landowner	Family of clothiers in Wotton-under-Edge	
1792-1797	**Edward Bearpacker** Owner **Shurmer Bath** Tenant	Quaker, maltster and property developer	1792 Shurmer Bath leases plot from Bearpacker, starts building cottage. 1793 Napoleonic Wars and housing slump.
1797-1812	**Ann** and **Frances Bearpacker** Owners **Shurmer Bath** Tenant (to 1800)	Clothiers	1797 site reverts to Bearpacker family. 1800 Shurmer Bath dies with £2,500 debts. Cottage then derelict?
1812/1813	**Jacob Crook senior** acquires site	Brewer	Jacob Crook senior buys two plots. "Ruinous cottage" already on site.
1813-1817	**Jacob Crook senior** Owner		Builds cottage and dwelling house on site.
1817-1819	**Hannah** and **Thomas Stroud** Residents **Jacob junior** and **Sarah Crook** Residents	Plumber/glazier Brewer	1819 Jacob Crook Snr dies, leaves whole property to wife Mary.
1819-1827	**Mary Crook** Owner Ditto as residents		1826 onwards disputed ownership
1827-1829	**Miss Phippen** Tenant **William Harrison** Tenant	Schoolmistress Leather factor	1829 Harrison declared bankrupt.
1829-1833	**Miss Phippen** Tenant **Hannah** and **Thomas Stroud** Residents		1832 William Beaumont accused of assaulting servant.
1833-1836	**Hannah** and **Thomas Stroud** Residents **William Beaumont** Tenant	Languages Professor	Beaumont runs languages academy by Bristol Bridge.
1836 - 1842	**Hannah** and **Thomas Stroud** Residents **William Watson** Tenant	Independent means	1842 ownership dispute settled, Jacob Crook jnr confirmed as owner.
1842-1850	**Jacob Crook jnr** Owner **William Watson** Tenant	Landed property	Jacob lives on upmarket Brandon Hill.
1850-1853	Owner ditto **Alfred Viner** Tenant	Hop merchant	1850 Alfred Viner runs business from home after bankruptcy. 1853 Alfred Viner dies.
1853-1861	Owner ditto **George Viner** Tenant	Brewing	
1861-1872	Owner ditto **George** and **Edward Viner** Tenants		1870 George Viner dies. 1872 Jacob Crook jnr dies, Spring Cottage property sold at auction.
1872-1879	**Henry Lee** Owner **Edward Viner** Tenant **Joseph and Harry Humphrey** Lodgers	Butcher Clerk Clerks	1870s start of increase in turnover of residents.
1879-1885	Owner ditto **Georgina Davis** Tenant	Houses and dividends	1885 Georgina Davis dies.
1885-1891	Owner ditto **Walter Vowles** Tenant **John B. McLaine** Tenant (1891)	Corn merchant Builder	1891 fire destroys Charles Franklin's glass works.

Period	Occupants	Occupation	Notes
1892-1898	Owner ditto **Charles Franklin** Tenant (1892-1893)	Mirror manufacturer	1893 John McLean convicted of assault on father-in-law. 1898 owner Henry Lee dies, leaves Spring Cottage to nephew.
1898-1905	**Henry Foot** Owner **William Moffatt** Tenant	Butcher Wire netting works superintendent	1898 land sold for three new terraced houses. 1901 child servant Ada Tovey employed by Moffatt family
1905-1909	Owner ditto **Alfred Warren** Tenant	Dickie, Parsons & Co (clothing firm) cashier	1909 Henry Foot gifts Spring Cottage to married daughter Clara.
1909-1925	**Clara Leigh** Owner **Alfred Warren** Tenant **Richard Ware** Tenant (1922-5)	Husband a salesman	1919 Evelyn Annie Warren on Social Study course at Bristol University. 1925 Ware buys house.
1925-1927	**Richard Ware** Owner-occupier	Fruit trade manager	Ware was first owner-occupier. 1927 house sold to Anton Sunderland.
1927-1928	**Anton Sunderland** Owner-occupier	Building contractor	1928 house sold to Ernest Herbert Fiddes.
1928-1935	**Ernest Herbert Fiddes** with wife **Minnie** Owner-occupier **William Bridgeman** Tenant	Shopkeeper/glass cutter Train driver	1930s influx of working class residents.
1935-1939	Owner-occupier and wife ditto **Harry Barton** Tenant	Upholsterer	1939 Harry and Ivy Barton's baby son Brian dies.
1939-1945	Owner-occupier and wife ditto		1942 son, also Ernest Fiddes, dies in sinking of submarine *Tempest*.
1945-1957	Owner-occupier and wife ditto **Betty Fiddes/Whitcombe** and **Maurice Whitcombe** Residents		1952 Betty Fiddes marries Maurice Whitcombe. 1957 owner Ernest Fiddes dies, leaves house to widow Minnie.
1957-1961	**Minnie Fiddes** Owner-occupier **Betty Whitcombe** Resident then owner-occupier **Maurice Whitcombe** Resident		1958 house sold to Betty Whitcombe. 1961 she sells to Jack and Mabel Coleman.
1961-1971	**Jack and Mabel Coleman** Owner-occupiers	Window blind manufacturer	Colemans are first joint owner-occupiers. 1971 Jack Coleman dies.
1971-1979	**Mabel Coleman** Owner-occupier **Guy and Geoffrey Coleman** adult sons, with daughter-in-law, Residents		1979 house sold to Penny Gane and Linda Hunter.
1979-1984	**Penny Gane** and **Linda Hunter** Joint owner-occupiers	School teachers	1984 house sold to Carolyn Britton.
1984-1986	**Carolyn Britton** Owner-occupier	University lecturer	1986 house sold to Peter and Sue Cullimore.
1986-present	**Peter and Sue Cullimore** Owner-occupiers	Radio/TV journalist Teacher and lecturer	1994 shed/stable made into living space. Penny Gane sets up Create Centre, chairs Bristol Women's Voice.

INTRODUCTION

A HOUSE THROUGH TIME

This book is about the many people who've lived in our house, 60 Fairfield Road, over the centuries. It's also about the men who built it and the mystery surrounding how old the house really is. Detailed advice is provided, too, for you the reader on how to research the history of your own home.

The project originates from when, in early 2019, a flyer was pushed through our door. It came from the producers of a TV history programme, *A House Through Time*. They were inviting my wife Sue and me to put forward our house as a candidate for their next series on BBC2, to be set in Bristol. We took up their offer and, to our amazement, eventually made the final shortlist for the series. In the end, 60 Fairfield Road wasn't the one chosen. But the experience inspired us to carry out a lot more research ourselves into the history of where we live and its past residents.

We were also building on previous discoveries by a local historian, Mary Wright, about 60 Fairfield Road. It followed the publication, in 2004, of her book on the history of Montpelier, entitled *Montpelier - a Bristol Suburb*. Back then, Mary cast an expert eye over our house deeds and gave us an initial summary, as well as a list of previous landowners before the house was built, and an account of the background to its construction.

Our narrative follows a broadly chronological pattern, from obscure eighteenth century origins up to the present day. We start with the property developers who built our home and how its quirky structure may have evolved. From then on, our main focus is on the lives of some of the 100 or so people who've resided there since its earliest times.

The kitchen of 60 Fairfield Road (photo: Paul Bullivant)

Inevitably, we had to be selective about which past residents to look at in detail. We chose only the most colourful and interesting characters, especially those about whom the most information was available. We're amazed at the rich variety of stories, all untold until now, that have emerged. There's an historical timeline at the start of the book, on page 4, to remind you who they all were and when they lived in the house.

Alongside their stories, you'll find information and guidance on researching the history of your own house and the people who lived in it before you. These sections, in the coloured boxes below and at the end of each chapter, outline the main sources of historical material which can serve the purpose.

The availability and range of sources change over time. So, with each chapter covering a particular period, the suggestions given are the most useful for researching house occupants of that era.

SHADOWY ORIGINS

We've always been intrigued by the unusual shape of our house. It was formerly known as Spring Cottage and stands on a hillside in Montpelier, which is a suburb designated as an historic conservation area on the north side of Bristol. The building looks big from outside, but this is an optical illusion – like a 'Tardis' in reverse.

It's long and thin, being only one room deep and really just a chain of rooms, with a staircase at each end. There are eight quite small rooms in total (plus an outbuilding now converted into living space) - four of them downstairs and the other four upstairs, in a similar linear formation.

60 Fairfield Road

There's plenty of evidence from our deeds of it having been built as two houses, attached but not connecting inside, and one older and smaller than the other. Until the 1960s the property was often referred to in official documents and other publications as "58 and 60 Fairfield Road", or with other variations in the numbering, or as "Spring Cottage" only. However, this name was not widely used until about 1840. Even after that it could sometimes mean just the old cottage, at other times the whole premises, or maybe even just the newer section. In the 1861 Census, the address was given as "Spring Villa".

The original small cottage, or oldest part, curves around the corner between Fairfield Road and the top of Old Ashley Hill. The rest, built in the early nineteenth century, adjoins it along Fairfield Road. It seems the two houses were blocked off from each other in those days, until inside access between them was opened up at an unknown later date. They weren't fully integrated into one home until the relatively recent past. It all adds up to a recipe for confusion and uncertainty that we've done our best to untangle accurately in this history. But it also makes for an exciting journey along the way.

60 Fairfield Road in spring 2020

The living room (Photo: Paul Bullivant)

HOW TO START RESEARCHING THE PEOPLE WHO LIVED IN YOUR HOUSE

Visit your local public Archives. You can find it through a Google search, or ask in your local library. You can often just turn up, or you may want to phone in advance to check that the material you want to look at is available. It's important to take with you any information you may have already. There could also be special workshops or talks about how to research people and places, given by archivists. Bristol Archives has a short written guide available. https://www.bristolmuseums.org.uk/bristol-archives/

Another good starting point is your house deeds, also known as title deeds. These might be lodged with your solicitor or the Land Registry, but you should be able to take a copy home if you request this. In the case of our Montpelier house, its deeds are unusually complete and therefore a great source. Deeds of old houses may also be kept in your local Archives.

Do you have any other information which might be useful in tracing past residents? Letters, photographs, even conversations with long-standing neighbours, may offer clues to more recent occupants. We were lucky enough to have one or two names and dates already to get us started. Most people will need to find them via a systematic search of records.

Local history books and pamphlets are a valuable source of background and contextual information. They may tell you more about what your neighbourhood was like when the house was built, and the social and economic changes since then. Local history societies are another rich source of information and support. Here you'll find like-minded and interested people, who may also offer help or advice with your research. Your local library will have details of all these avenues.

Anything else you can find out, like how past residents of your house made a living, or when extensions were added, may also be helpful initially. You can then start building on this information to discover more about the social history of your house, as will be shown in the following chapters.

CHAPTER I

EIGHTEENTH CENTURY

SHURMER BATH - FIRST DEVELOPER

Our house deeds and other official records indicate that Shurmer Bath (1738-1800), a businessman from nearby Stokes Croft, started building a cottage on our site as part of a larger housing development, but may never have completed it. He leased 23 acres of meadow land, of which ours was less than one acre, from wealthy landowner Edward Bearpacker in 1792.

Bearpacker came from a prominent family of clothiers in Wotton-under-Edge, a Cotswold wool town about 15 miles north in Gloucestershire. He had been buying up land in the Montpelier area. In the late 1780s, Bearpacker started dividing the land into plots and leasing it to developers, including Shurmer Bath.[1]

The latter agreed to pay an annual rent of £300 and to complete within five years *"so many good, substantial and uniform houses of stout brick and timber that should secure the £300 yearly income"*.[2]

However, from about 1794, all Bath's building work on what was to become Spring Cottage, and on other nearby new houses, had to stop in the slump caused by France declaring war on Britain. The Napoleonic Wars followed, and carried on intermittently until 1815, with all the country's resources needed for the conflict. One of our deeds states that in 1812 a *"ruinous cottage"* stood on our site in upper Montpelier.

As Shurmer Bath ran up large debts, the land use reverted to the Bearpacker family (by now Edward's daughters Ann and Frances) in 1797. However, there's evidence that Bath may have lived in the cottage, even if it wasn't completed.

In several of our deeds he's listed as the property's first tenant, with the

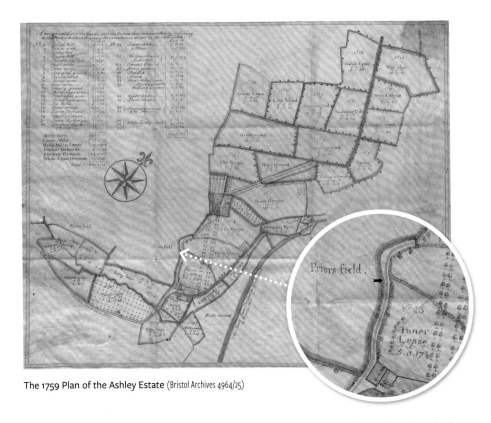

The 1759 Plan of the Ashley Estate (Bristol Archives 4964/25)

house and garden formerly *"in the occupation of Shurmer Bath"*. When he died in 1800, aged 61, he still owed the Bearpackers £2,500.

A legal settlement document between the Bearpacker sisters and Shurmer Bath's heirs (his daughters Mary and Elizabeth) in 1809 explained the impact of the financial collapse on him:

"Shurmer Bath ....erected on part of the before mentioned premises several messuages [houses] or tenements and other buildings and was in great forwarding of completing many others and fulfilling his covenants and engagements until the unexpected alteration of things by the....war with France and the failure of a plan then in contemplation for erecting various other messuages and buildings on the said premises which had subjected the said Shurmer Bath to great inconveniences and much loss and left him unable to perform the whole of the said rented covenants". [3]

All these documents are frustratingly vague about land distribution, exactly when and where the new houses were built and how many. Shurmer Bath is thought to have planned his housing development on four "closes" (divided-up fields) of around five acres each, which later became part of Fairfield, York, Richmond and Cobourg Roads.

However, one can surmise by comparing a local map, the 1759 Plan of the Ashley Estate, with later maps of Bristol, that our original cottage was built on the extreme eastern edge of an adjoining estate, Priors Field. (See the page opposite). The plan was drawn in 1759 to show the estate as it had been when it was sold in 1731. Our site, probably not yet built on, is towards the bottom left, just above the crook of a big dogleg bend in the field layout, and approximately where the name Priors Field can be deciphered.

The 1828 Ashmead map (see page 16) was the first detailed one to include Montpelier, which still lay in Gloucestershire and wasn't incorporated into Bristol until 1832.

SHURMER BATH - A MAN OF MANY PARTS

Apart from being a businessman and property developer, Shurmer Bath was a prominent Quaker and well-known local philanthropist. In the Quaker birth, marriage and death records for Bristol, there's a hand-written birth certificate, signed by two midwives, which gives his date of birth as 29 October 1738. According to the certificate, Shurmer was born in Barton Street (in Stokes Croft), at the home of his parents, James and Sarah Bath. He was the middle one of five brothers and sisters.

James Bath was a maltster, and Shurmer later became one too, eventually taking over the family business. They made malt from barley or other grain for brewing beer. Before that, aged just 16, Shurmer went to London in 1755 as an apprentice to a patten maker by the name of Josiah Hoskins, who was also his brother-in-law and a fellow Quaker.[4] Pattens were wooden under-shoes for outdoors to lift you above the muddy streets.

Josiah Hoskins had married Shurmer's older sister Elizabeth in London five years earlier, when Josiah was 21 and she was 19. At that young age, Elizabeth needed parental consent, which may have been lacking as the ceremony is listed in London's Clandestine Marriage Register for that period. Quaker records show the couple both died young, in their thirties, from *"consumption"*, or tuberculosis.

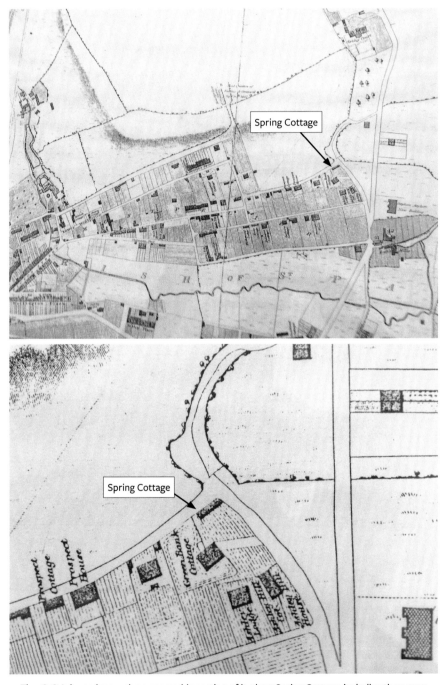

The 1828 Ashmead map, plus a zoomed-in section of it, show Spring Cottage, including the newer build, on the edge of open fields. (Know Your Place/Bristol Archives 04481)

Shurmer's younger brother, Nevil Bath, who was his junior by 10 years, became a cutler in the Redcliff (now spelt Redcliffe) area of Bristol. At his work premises in Redcliff Street, he made not only cutlery but also surgical instruments and toys. Nevil lived in prosperous Clifton for much of his adult life.

Shurmer Bath must also have been commercially successful, in his case as a maltster, (until he over-reached himself much later as a housing developer), since he could afford charity for Bristol's poor.

An obituary in The Monthly Magazine, after his death in 1800, offered the following tribute:

Shurmer was *"commonly called Dr Bath from his dispensing large quantities of medicine to the poor gratis. One of the principal promoters of the Bristol Asylum for the Blind, of the Schools of St James and St Paul and of other charitable institutions in the city, he was a man of a humane and benevolent disposition."* [5]

SHURMER BATH THE WRITER

We've found no portrait or drawing of "Dr Bath". However, an authentic record does exist of the man expressing himself in his own words. In 1796 he wrote an eight-page preface to a book of sermons, based on the Old Testament, by a 12-year-old Bristol girl, Charlotte Rees. Shurmer described her as a *"poetical genius"* whose *"extraordinary talents"* deserved to be widely known.[6]

The Quaker businessman was a friend of Charlotte's family, also Quakers, who had become impoverished through a tragic misfortune. In the preface he wrote that Charlotte had *"respectable and deserving parents, with minds adapted to a more favorable rank in life; but losses, disappointments and treacherous connections exposed the family to very severe trials. Her father, at an early period, after he was bereft of his property, sunk under his afflictions, and left her mother with five daughters in such distress as called for the most firm reliance on divine protection."*

This could almost be a description also of Shurmer's own recent misfortune. He, too, was "bereft of his property" after his disastrous foray into house building in Montpelier. Charlotte's parents, not named in the preface, were David Rees, a wine merchant, and his wife Elizabeth.

Shurmer related how, in 1793, Charlotte's family had been *"brought under my notice by the very severe indispositions of two of the daughters"*. This must be an example of the maltster being known also as an unofficial doctor, giving out free medicine to the poor, as portrayed in his obituary.

The preface also explained that Shurmer and other Quaker benefactors had been gathering subscriptions to publish Charlotte's sermons, which he praised for *"the scriptural piety they breathe throughout. The just attachment the authoress manifests towards many of the great doctrines of Christianity, such as the divinity of our blessed Lord and Saviour...shew her to be farther advanced in the school of religion than could have been expected from a child of her age."*

Shurmer tells us that Charlotte had also written over 60 poems in her short lifetime. He added this poignant message at the end of his preface to *Sermons*:

"N.B. If this specimen of Charlotte's abilities should excite in the breasts of the Subscribers a desire to be made acquainted with her Poems, it is intended to publish them in one volume."

The child prodigy grew up to marry William Lloyd, a tea dealer, in 1817. Sadly, though, her life was to be cut short. Charlotte died just a year later, at the age of only 36.

Shurmer's contribution to the book of sermons speaks volumes about his character. It reveals a well-educated, kind and sensitive man, who was also deeply religious in his beliefs and dedicated to helping others (especially if they were Quakers). Even more amazing is that he wrote the preface just after being ruined himself while trying to build our house.

SHURMER BATH AND THE SLAVE TRADE

However, there's another side to Shurmer Bath's life which gives a rather different picture. He married twice and developed close links with the slave trade through each of his wives, who were related to one another.

According to the Quaker records, his first wife Mary, whom he married in January 1767, was the daughter of John Lewis, *"late of the Island of Barbados, planter, deceased, and Elizabeth his wife"*. It's a logical assumption that Shurmer's late father-in-law John Lewis must, therefore, have owned slaves.

Tragically for Shurmer and Mary, their married life together lasted just

'Cutting the Sugar Cane' [in Antigua], painted by William Clark, 1823 (Image: Spartacus Educational)

one year. She died in, or soon after, childbirth and was buried in January 1768 at Quakers Friars in central Bristol. But the couple's newborn daughter, also Mary, survived.

The Quaker records show that Shurmer then remarried in April 1771, again to a slave owner's daughter. His second wife, Alice, was the daughter of Andrew Dury, a Quaker merchant in Bristol, and Mary Dury.

Andrew Dury had owned at least one sugar plantation, again in Barbados, with 50 slaves, but sold up for the large sum of £8,300. (This was the equivalent of around £1.7 million in today's money.) He moved to Bristol in 1763, when Alice was about 16. This was at a time when the Quaker movement was encouraging its members to disinvest from slavery.

The Dury family had lived in St Peter's, Barbados, for a century and owned a lot of property in the island's Speightstown area. Both they and the Lewises were related by marriage to the Morrises - a family of brewers and

Quakers, originally from London, who had emigrated to America and settled in Philadelphia.

The source for all this information is *The Morris Family of Philadelphia Descendants of Anthony Morris 1654-1721*, a book written by Robert Charles Moon and published in 1908.[7] This Morris family archive includes a reproduction of a conveyance document for the sale of Andrew Dury's plantation:

> **DEED—Barbados.**
> **ANDREW DURY** of St. Peter's, Barbados, and Mary his wife, convey to Stephen Welch of the Town of Speight, Merchant, for the consideration of £8300 a sugar work plantation in the said parish, containing 89 acres, 3 roods, 21 perches, bounding on the lands of the Honble. Sir John Gibbons, Baronet, and John Caddle, on lands late of Henry Anderson, and Dr. Alexander Ross, deceased, on lands belonging to said parish of St. Peter, called the Free School, and of John Archer, and on lands late of Saml. Battally, Esq., deceased, with the windmill, dwelling house, boyling house, still house and all other houses. The purchase also includes another piece of land containing 19 acres, 1 rood, 36 perches in the same parish, bounding on parish land called the Free School, on lands of Thomas Williams, on the Broad Road, on lands of Wm. Bruton, Prudence Phillips, lands of late Henry Anderson and John Bycroft, deceased, on the Bowling Alley and lands of Thomas Maddox ; also 50 negros, all utensils and 40 head of cattle.
> **ANDREW DURY.**

Extract from the Morris Family of Philadelphia archive. The final phrase tells us the sale included "50 negros, all utensils and 40 head of cattle".

The sale was completed on 21 August 1762. The Morris archive adds that, on the same date, Andrew Dury and his wife Mary sold to Stephen Welsh (the same buyer) "*10 slaves for the sum of £450*".

Andrew and Mary Dury sailed back to Bristol in a large group of 16 family members, including children and other relatives. The archive also reveals that the women who later became Shurmer Bath's first and second wives, Mary Lewis and Alice Dury, were in fact cousins. They travelled back together from Barbados as part of that family group. Mary's father, the plantation owner John Lewis (who died in 1747), had married Andrew Dury's sister, Elizabeth.

SHURMER THE QUAKER MOVER AND SHAKER

According to the Quaker records, guests at Shurmer and Alice's wedding, in Bristol in 1771, included numerous members of the Fry family. Many of the same would also attend his funeral 30 years later at the Quaker burial ground opposite St Mary Redcliffe Church. It was a significant tribute to the maltster from Bristol's Quaker industrial hierarchy.

Shurmer Bath (1738-1800) was a contemporary of Joseph Fry (1728-1787), who turned chocolate manufacturing into a major industry for the city, well known across Britain and far beyond. The two men knew each other via their Quaker and business links. Shurmer also rubbed shoulders with many Fry family members involved in a variety of other trades. However, when Shurmer's father-in-law, Andrew Dury, died on 14 November 1784, it was the original chocolate maker himself, Joseph Fry, who signed the death certificate as registrar to the Bristol Monthly Meeting.

Andrew Dury's death registration was signed by fellow Quaker and chocolate manufacturer Joseph Fry in November 1784. (Image: Quaker Records)

Although in the eighteenth century Quakers formed only a tiny minority in the population as a whole, Bristol was a stronghold for them. A disproportionate number of the city's most successful merchants and financiers emerged from the Society of Friends, as Quakers were also known. In the seventeenth century, they had faced persecution because of their refusal to participate in the established Church or fight for their country. Quakers believe each individual has a direct and personal relationship with God. In Bristol well-heeled Friends helped each other and made charitable donations, while encouraging courtesy, frugality and hard work among their employees.[8]

Many of these businessmen took their religious beliefs and duties very seriously and, like the Frys, played an active, sometimes even bureaucratic, role in the Quaker community.

The Morris archive tells us that Shurmer Bath, too, was an active member of the Society of Friends in Bristol throughout his adult life. When still a young businessman, he attended their regular Monthly Meetings and sat on the men's committee.

In the 1760s the latter comprised 27 prominent *"men-Friends"* (a description given them by the archive.) As well as Shurmer Bath, they included Andrew Dury, John P. Fry and John's father, William Fry, who was a grocer and acted as clerk to the committee.

The Morris archive quotes from the minutes at one of the men's committee meetings in 1765. Andrew Dury was going on a business trip to North America, and requested a certificate from the Bristol Friends as an introduction to American Quaker contacts.

Shurmer Bath and a colleague were *"desired to make the necessary enquiries concerning him and prepare a certificate for the approbation of our next meeting"*. This happened while Shurmer was still married to his first wife, Mary.[9]

The same archive tells us that a few years later, in 1778, Hannah Dury, a sister of Shurmer's second wife Alice, married John P. Fry at the Friars Meeting House in Bristol.

Although in the 1760s Bristol was still second only to Liverpool as a slaving port, the city's predominance in the slave trade had ended and the trade was already in decline. In her book *Slavery Obscured*, Madge Dresser points out that Quakers in Bristol had long been significantly involved in it, but at the

The eighteenth century former Friends' Meeting House at Quakers Friars, Bristol, where Shurmer Bath married each of his wives, Mary Lewis and Alice Dury, in 1767 and 1771. (Photo: Paul Bullivant)

same time influential local Friends were now pressurising them to withdraw.

Dresser found evidence of this from meetings of the men's committee of which Shurmer Bath became a member. She quotes from the minutes at one meeting, on 4 January 1762, after a deputation of four men had been instructed *"to inquire if any Friend is concerned in the Negro Trade"*.

The deputation reported: *"It appears that only one Friend is actually concerned in the African Trade who soon proposes to sell out and to have no connection with it."* [10]

Were they referring to Shurmer Bath's future father-in-law, Andrew Dury? He did, indeed, sell his plantation in Barbados, just seven months later. (See pages 19-20.)

Shurmer Bath was already the father of one girl, Mary, when he married his second wife, Alice Dury, in 1771. She bore him three more daughters. They were: Sarah, who was born in June 1773 and died in 1803, aged 29; Elizabeth, born in November 1774 and still living in 1809; and Hannah, who lived for only 10 months after her birth in May 1776.

Alice died in 1809, when still residing in Stokes Croft, presumably in the Bath family home at number 93. There's no evidence of her ever inhabiting our house in Montpelier – except that she was married to Shurmer. He probably did live there some time in the 1790s, but for how long and until when is still unknown.

Two years before Alice's death, on 25 March 1807, the Abolition of the Slave Trade Act had finally been given the royal assent. This abolished the slave trade in the British colonies and made it illegal for enslaved people to be carried on British ships.

SHURMER BATH – THE MAN IN FULL

There was even more to Shurmer Bath than we've seen up to this point. Indeed, the fuller truth about him would have eluded us completely, had it not been for a chance conversation with the City Archivist for Bristol. She guided us to a volume in Bristol Archives' own collection. *The Diary of Sarah Fox, née Champion,1745-1802*, makes over 20 references to Shurmer Bath and offers a unique personal insight into a man the diarist knew well for 40 years.[11]

Sarah Champion, who married later in life, was another well-to-do Bristol Quaker. From about 20 until middle age, she lived with her brother Richard Champion, a porcelain manufacturer, and his family at their home near the factory on Castle Green. Sarah kept a regular diary for much of her life, in which she described her activities and innermost thoughts in vivid detail.

Sarah recorded meeting Shurmer Bath for the first time on 12 January 1761, when she was 18 years old and he was 22. It happened in the parlour of Joseph Fry's house in Narrow Wine Street. Both had been invited there to spend the evening. She wrote afterwards:

"Here I met with Shurmer Bath, a young man celebrated for the goodness of his understanding and command of temper in argument. With him I had some conversation – principally on stage entertainments, of the impropriety of which he convinced me." [12]

On 1 October 1782, Sarah's diary reports, she visited a friend's house to find Shurmer *"trying the effect of electricity on CP* [Catherine Phillips, a Quaker female preacher] *who had an increasing stiffness in her joints"*. [13]

We're not told what this experiment entailed or if it worked. However, the entry indicates that "Dr Bath" was acquainted with the latest scientific ideas – and perhaps even ahead of his time in relation to electricity.

Benjamin Franklin, the American scientist and inventor, had previously carried out experiments in pain relief in the mid eighteenth century, using an early form of battery. Electrotherapy was now being popularised, mainly by unqualified doctors, for a range of medical conditions.

This could even involve an "electric bath" to build up a high voltage charge in the patient's body, so that it was "bathed", not in water, but in electricity. The treatment was painless, but could literally make your hair stand on end.[14]

Hannah More, who sought Shurmer Bath's advice on setting up schools. Portrait by John Opie (1761-1807). (Image: Girton College, University of Cambridge)

Following Sarah Champion's diary entry in 1782, it would be a further 17 years before a young Humphry Davy experimented with nitrous oxide gas as a therapeutic treatment at the Pneumatic Institute in Clifton, then with electricity at the Royal Institution in London.[15]

Shurmer Bath was a frequent visitor to the Champion household for many years. After Sarah invited his eldest daughter Mary for tea, she commented in the diary: *"We were much pleased with her."*

As for Shurmer's lifestyle with his second wife, Alice: *"Their manner of living was very retired, but he was much among his friends and his company sought after, his conversation being generally entertaining."*

The diary also reveals that Shurmer knew some of the leading reformers of the age. On 3 January 1789 he, Sarah and others spent an evening with Thomas Clarkson, the anti-slavery campaigner. His participation suggests that, by then, despite the slave-owning background of his in-laws, Shurmer had become an abolitionist.[16]

In September 1789 Sarah reported: *"My brother brought home Hannah More, Sally and Patty.* [The latter two were pet names for Hannah's sisters Sarah and Martha.] *Shurmer was sent for to whom they wanted to talk about the schools they wished to establish in the neighbourhood."* [17]

Hannah's sisters had opened a school for girls from affluent families in 1758 at College Green, later transferring it to larger premises in Park Street.[18] Just a month after their consultation with Shurmer, Hannah More opened an early Sunday school in Cheddar with Patty. It was the first of a dozen such schools they established in the Mendip area by 1800. The great social reformer and campaigner had thought it worth seeking the advice of Shurmer Bath before going ahead. Indeed, he did have some expertise in education, too.

SHURMER THE SCHOOL BENEFACTOR

In early 1790 Shurmer helped to set up the Friends School Bristol at Quakers Friars. He sat on the school committee, and headed a list of 22 Quaker subscribers who attended their first meeting on 9 April, with Shurmer donating £50 himself. It's worth noting this appears to have been his one and only financial contribution. Soon afterwards he began his ruinous investment in land development in Montpelier that cost him so dear.

The school rules were made available as a printed pamphlet. It declared their aim was to provide a free day school, run by a salaried Master, for 30 boys *"of such Parents as may not be of ability to give them the necessary learning"*. The children all had to be *"members of the religious society of the people called Quakers"* and adhere to their moral code.

The curriculum focused on reading, writing and arithmetic. All pupils should be clean and punctual and must *"avoid quarrelling, striking or teasing one another, avoid gaming of all kinds, using the Sacred Name irreverently, mocking the aged and deformed"*.

After 10 years the school began accepting girls, to be taught in a separate adjoining room. However, it did so only because it was struggling to enrol enough boys.[19]

Shurmer was also a prime backer of much larger new "benevolent" schools for the parishes of St James and St Paul, sited where the St James Barton roundabout (known locally as the "Bearpit") is today. From 1790 hundreds of boys and girls from poor families were *"daily taught Reading, Sewing & c; cloathed for Divine Worship once a year and conducted by the Masters and Mistresses every*

This postcard, based on an early engraving of the School (or "Asylum") for the Blind, shows inmates working – boys making baskets and girls spinning. On the far right, a customer appears to be buying a finished basket. (Image: courtesy of Bristol Culture, Bristol Museum & Art Gallery)

Sunday to St James's Church". A separate school just for girls opened in 1794.[20]

Shurmer Bath's most lasting achievement, though, (apart from a section of our house), was to set up the Bristol School for the Blind, or "Asylum", in 1793. The school trained visually impaired people for future employment. They specialised in crafts like basket and mat making, the best of which were sold to the public. In the nineteenth century it was sited at the top of Park Street, roughly where the Wills Memorial Building stands now. The Blind School didn't finally close until 1968.[21]

That Shurmer Bath was the main founder has been revealed in the *Diary of Sarah Fox*. In her entry for 18 February 1793, Sarah, (now married to the banker Charles Fox), wrote:

"The blind school was opened, to which I paid a very pleasing visit. This useful institution was begun by Shurmer Bath, who persuaded my husband to join him in active service to become Treasurer. Two girls, about 14 years old, were the first pupils; there was also a little boy, and 2 more were soon added." [22]

Much of this deep involvement in local schools took place while Shurmer had teams of builders trying to finish our house, and others, to meet his contractual obligations as Britain prepared for war against France.

SHURMER BATH - FINAL RECKONING

Even when Shurmer faced heavy debts, the hyperactive maltster wasn't quite finished yet. In February 1798, according to Sarah's diary, he was still doing his philanthropic medical work, and had even extended it to the city of Bath. She complained of him neglecting his church duties as a result:

"He kept lodgings at Bath to receive patients. Many of his friends regretted that so much of his time was thus occupied, as it not only deprived them of his society but of his watchfulness in the Church, as well as of his attendance at meetings for worship." [23]

In the following year, however, Shurmer began to fade. On 1 June 1799, Sarah Fox and her husband joined him at an anniversary celebration for the schools at St James's Barton. They watched *"the children of the Parish Schools... assembled in Portland Square and some of them and the Blind Children at dinner... It seemed to create general concern that Shurmer Bath looked so ill as to almost exclude a hope of his being present at another anniversary."* [24]

Exactly a year later, on 1 June, Sarah's diary recorded her being at home in Brunswick Square after dinner. *"Shurmer Bath entered – the almost shadow of what he once was – yellow, emaciated and hardly able to move."*[25]

Shurmer finally died on 26 July 1800. As Sarah mourned her friend, the diary again put her thoughts into words: *"It is now 40 years since I was first acquainted with him, and many were the hours in time passed, I have enjoyed his interesting conversation."*

At his burial on 30 July, Sarah was there, along with a large crowd of mourners, on a blisteringly hot day: *"I attended with my husband (but not as invited guests) the funeral of our deceased friend at Redclift burying ground. It drew together great numbers. The blind school and two or three other schools attended to pay the last tribute of respect to the memory of their benefactor."*[26]

It seems this complex and multi-talented man, who reached out beyond the Quaker community, was highly popular among rich and poor alike. Shurmer Bath was also highly successful in many ways and suffered only one big failure - his attempt to build houses in Montpelier.

But he was no saint. Shurmer laid the foundations of his wealth by twice marrying into a slave owner's family, after they sold up in the Caribbean.

RESEARCHING THE PEOPLE WHO LIVED IN YOUR HOUSE BEFORE 1800

Pre-1800 is more difficult to research than post-1800 because there's usually less documentary evidence available. The national 10-yearly Census didn't begin until 1841, although early incomplete records were made from 1801. So, to find out about earlier residents, you will need other sources. One possibility may be local poll books, which listed all voters and gave their approximate address. In Bristol these records cover the period 1715 to 1847, but there are gaps.

Usually, the first step will be to seek people's names, ages and dates of birth. The **title deeds** of your house can be a good place to start finding clues. However, deeds are often incomplete and don't mention all the occupants over time. They name only those involved in changes of ownership or other legal transactions, plus some tenants if they were head of household. The occupants might also have included their wives, children and other family members, or tenants, lodgers and servants, but all of these were likely to be ignored in the documents. Other evidence is usually needed to identify them.

Some useful information on house occupants can be found **online**, through websites such as **Ancestry** https://www.ancestry.co.uk/ or **Find My Past** https://www.findmypast.co.uk/. Baptisms, marriages and burials were recorded before 1800. However, it's difficult to identify house occupants on Ancestry until the first Census in 1841. Parish records left out addresses and rarely gave birth or death details. Your best chance of identification is by seeking links with other family members. Another problem is that parish names and boundaries may have changed over time, likewise how the names of people, houses and streets are spelt. House numbering only became established in the nineteenth century. All this can make searching a time-consuming but addictive process, sometimes involving a wild goose chase or dead end. These genealogy websites do charge a fee to register, so it may be worth waiting until you have some initial clues before signing up. However, **Ancestry can be used free of charge** in any of Bristol's public libraries (and many others elsewhere), also in the searchroom at Bristol Archives.

Examples of the type of material held in Bristol Archives or your local **Archives or Records Office** for researching pre-1800 people are:

1. **Land ownership and legal transaction documents** for individual properties and lands, like the 1759 Plan of the Ashley Lands, which helped us locate the site of Spring Cottage before it was built.

2. **Taxes, rates, surveys and valuations documents** may be useful in providing clues about who lived in the house and/or who owned it at that time. Some taxes, such as the Hearth Tax in the seventeenth century, were paid by the occupants, who were taxed on each of their hearths. The Window Tax was a similar levy from the late 1600s until its repeal in 1851. Bristol Archives, for example, holds records of these, as well as for Land Tax on many pre-1800 buildings in the city. Poor Rate books show who paid tax as a contribution to relief of the poor in Bristol, from 1698 onwards.

3. **Archives of local organisations** may include documents relevant to individuals who lived in the house. For example, these could be about early schools (like the ones funded by Shurmer Bath), or organisations which the occupants belonged to, like the Quakers' Society of Friends, trades societies or guilds, clubs and movements. The Quakers kept extensive and detailed records going back to at least 1700.

4. **Old maps and plans** showing the land on which the house was built and the surrounding area as it became developed for housing. You may find clues about the past local economy and social organisation by studying the maps for industrial buildings, churches, orchards, farms, etc, which perhaps are now gone. These can shed light on the lives of residents in your house over time. The Archives staff will show you what's available. However, accurate street maps of Bristol weren't produced until the early nineteenth century.

5. **Books, journals, newspapers, diaries and pamphlets** relevant to investigating the past residents of your house. These may not be accessible in their original form except via an Archives centre or library.

An example is the *Diary of Sarah Fox*, which provided a glimpse into the everyday world of Shurmer Bath and his contemporaries. However, that diary can also be read online and downloaded. Newspapers can be searched in the reference section of Bristol Central Library, or online. Sources like these will be explored in later chapters, when they become more significant.

You can search the **Bristol Archives catalogue** at http://archives.bristol. co.uk , or in their public searchroom, for items relevant to your research. Or explore the online services of your own local Archives by finding their website.

Other very useful sources for pre-1800 research are:

Know Your Place: http://www.kypwest.org.uk/, a free online resource which is well worth exploring for the West of England. It's a digital mapping project, providing a series of interactive historical maps and information layers, including photographs. These can be overlaid on one another to build up a fuller, more detailed, picture of the selected area over time. Historical and contemporary information is always being added to these maps. They currently cover most of the West Country and other areas are joining in.

Google searches. Just a simple search, using people's names, place names or any other information you have, is definitely worth trying. In our case the 1796 *Sermons*, by Charlotte Rees, popped up as a Google Book during a general trawl for references to Shurmer Bath.

Library books can provide a great deal of background, and sometimes specific, detail about the people in your house before 1800. Your local **public library** will help you navigate their catalogue, but you may also be able to do this online. University libraries hold extensive collections of books, journals and other materials in their special collections. You can usually do a basic catalogue search online and then visit the **university library** to read the material. Ask about photocopying and other public access services.

The **National Archive** http://discovery.nationalarchives.gov.uk, the **British Library** https://www.bl.uk/, and many specialist archives and collections, may be the next steps if you get really carried away on your trail!

CHAPTER 2
EARLY NINETEENTH CENTURY

JACOB CROOK – FATHER AND SON

Our title deeds reveal that Jacob Crook (1769 – 1819), who was a *"common brewer"* in Narrow Wine Street in the city centre, built the larger part of our house. A conveyance document from 1898 states that Spring Cottage was *"erected, built and laid out by Jacob Crook on a piece of meadow pasture, or arable land"*.

Crook bought the land in two separate stages. Another legal document in the deeds tells us that, in March 1812, he paid the Bearpacker sisters £206 for *"2 roods"* [about half an acre] of garden ground, *"whereon a ruinous cottage or hut was then standing...then in the occupation of said Jacob Crook"*. In December 1813, Crook then paid the Bearpackers £104 for a smaller piece of adjoining pasture, measuring 80 feet by 80 feet.

Was the *"ruinous cottage"* built 20 years before, then lived in, by Shurmer Bath? Or was it the remains of a much older house? A third possibility is that both are true - that Bath built onto a derelict existing cottage and Jacob Crook later added a larger extension.

Shurmer Bath died in 1800, and the deeds state several times that he was a *"tenant"* or *"occupied"* the property. This implies there had been some sort of dwelling on the site before 1800, and Bath lived in it. Unfortunately, the deeds do not specify when, why, or for how long.

Since the *"ruinous cottage"* was already *"in the occupation of said Jacob Crook"* when the latter bought his first piece of land in 1812, Crook may also have lived in it himself before and/or during his own building work. However, there could be some ambiguity in the often obtuse legal jargon used at the time.

The house deeds refer to "a ruinous cottage" already standing on Jacob Crook's plot in 1812

HOUSING SLUMP

Why would Shurmer Bath, as a prosperous member of Bristol's Quaker business community, choose to live in what must have been little more than a hovel on the very edge of the city? After all, Shurmer had married into a well-off family, the Durys, who had made a small fortune from the slave trade.

However, it does become somewhat more credible when you bear in mind that here was a man who had been ruined by the sudden collapse of the housing market. Perhaps a *"ruinous cottage"* was now all he could afford. Another possibility is that he set up a temporary home on the building site, to supervise construction of the house and all his others nearby.

The following vivid picture of a 'boom and bust' scenario in the 1790s, involving not just Shurmer Bath but also other developers across the city, is given by John Latimer's *Annals of Bristol in the Eighteenth Century*. It was first published from the perspective of a century later, in 1893.

"A terrace of 60 houses, to cost £60,000, was proposed to be built near Ashley Down.....The mania had scarcely burst into full bloom before it evinced signs of coming decay..... On the breaking out of the French war, in 1793, there was a financial panic throughout the kingdom, and the failure of Messrs. Lockier, McAulay

and Co, the most extensive of the local speculators, heralded the ruin of a crowd of minor firms."

Latimer's account continues: *"More than 600 houses [across Bristol] in course of construction were left unfinished, and the appearance of the suburbs, for many years after this collapse, reminded strangers of a place that had undergone bombardment. The shells of thirty-four roofless houses stood in York Crescent, the Mall, Saville Place, Belle Vue, Richmond Place, York Place and other localities."*

He concludes: *"Kingsdown and St Michael's Hill presented many mournful wrecks; Portland Square and the neighbouring streets were in the same condition; and Great George Street and its environs were in no better plight."* [27]

ARCHITECTURAL PUZZLE

Although nowhere in Montpelier is mentioned in Latimer's account, our site stands less than a mile from Portland Square, Kingsdown and Ashley Down, which he names among the districts worst hit by the slump. Around the time of Waterloo in 1815, or within a couple of years either side, Jacob Crook seems to have built a new and larger house onto a cottage that was already there, while retaining the older building's original structure.

The old and new parts were always joined together, but it seems that at first there was no through access from one to the other. Each dwelling had a separate entrance door from the garden side, and their tiled roofs are pitched at right angles to each other. The evidence suggests that Jacob wanted two separate homes on the site, but with an option to unify them easily later on.

The cottage end of our house must originally have been a two-up two-down. It has much thicker walls than the rest, a tiny separate staircase, narrower doorways, and smaller rooms of a very different style and, it appears, age.

It's also possible that the *"ruinous cottage or hut"* mentioned in our deeds had, by 1812, become a one-up one-down, because part of it had collapsed. Some evidence for this can again be deduced from the structure. The end room of the original cottage is on a lower level than the rest of our house as it stands today, both on the ground floor and, especially, above. Here, you go down two steps, or about half a metre, to access the upstairs bathroom. This seems more than necessary to compensate for sloping ground at the top of Old Ashley

Staircase in the original cottage

Staircase in the newer part of the house (Photos: Paul Bullivant)

The back of our house shows the newer part in the foreground and the original cottage at the far end.
(Photo: Paul Bullivant)

There's a drop of half a metre down to the top end room. (Photo: Paul Bullivant)

Hill. It may also be another sign that extensions were added later.

However, the most compelling evidence for our 'collapse and re-build' theory is found outside. The 3D satellite image of 60 Fairfield Road on Google Earth shows a roof with three separate sections, the largest built at right angles to the others. (See the image on page 38.)

The old cottage end of the house has two parallel roofs of contrasting shape and pitch. The far roof is shallow, whereas the other is pitched - but unevenly - to form a rough 'V' between them. It suggests that when Shurmer Bath started his building work, in about 1793, a cottage already

Google Earth 3D satellite image of 60 Fairfield Road in November 2019

The oldest part of our house downstairs is now a bathroom. We think it was originally the kitchen, because of its deep, built-in, cupboard space. (Photo: Paul Bullivant)

stood in that corner of the site. However, it was in such a bad state that he had to demolish about half of it, re-build onto the more solid furthest end, and put on a new roof alongside the old one. Then war intervened and Shurmer never completed the job.

When Jacob Crook bought the plot in 1812, that unfinished structure from 20 years earlier – itself perhaps built onto something considerably older – could have been the *"ruinous cottage or hut"* referred to in our deeds. Crook then, no doubt, had to carry out a major restoration of that building. It may even have been he, rather than Bath, who laid the pitched roof, before adding the long extension that formed a second, adjoining, house.

In her book on the history of Montpelier, Mary Wright says several other owners of Georgian houses nearby believe theirs were also built in more than one stage over time.[28] In our case, there's reason to believe it happened in at least four stages:

1. A two-up, two-down cottage of uncertain age was built on a slope.
2. In the early 1790s, Shurmer Bath wholly, or partially, demolished the two rooms that stood on higher ground, one directly above the other, because they were crumbling.
3. Bath started re-building this part of the cottage, but never finished.
4. In the early 1800s, Jacob Crook completed the re-build, then added his extension.

Most excitingly of all, it would mean the two end rooms nearest Old Ashley Hill, nowadays used as upstairs and downstairs bathrooms, pre-date Shurmer Bath and were built earlier in the eighteenth century.

STRANGE BREWER

We found a clue in the deeds which seems completely at odds with all the other facts and figures given in them. A document of 1898 reviews the timeline of previous legal agreements drawn up in the ownership history of Spring Cottage.[29]

The mysterious reference to 1776 is in the top line of this extract from a legal document of 1898.

First on the list is a clear one-line statement: "*15 December 1776 Indre [Indenture] of Conveyance between J Crook of the one part and Wm Harrison of the other part*".

In other words, some sort of transaction involving a Jacob Crook and another man over the Spring Cottage site took place as early as 1776 – with even the exact date specified.

However, another legal document in our deeds gives precisely the same day and month for a conveyance agreement, also between two people called Jacob Crook and William Harrison, but 50 years later – on 15 December 1826!

By 1826, Crook had died. But we know from the deeds an agreement really did happen that year, and on that very day. It involved Crook's son, also named Jacob, illegally selling his half share in the property to Harrison. The latter was a leather merchant who went bankrupt.

Jacob Crook, the father, died in November 1819, aged 50. Therefore, he was just a child at the time of the conveyance agreement in 1776, and couldn't have been the J. Crook involved in that deal. Was it Jacob senior's own father, perhaps signing an agreement with Harrison's father? Or did the lawyers give the wrong year by a slip of the pen, intending to write 1826? It seems very unlikely, however, they would make such a gross error in a legal document. Unless this discrepancy can be solved, we'll never find out for sure how old our house is.

60 Fairfield Road in summer 2019

TWO HOUSES

Another document from our deeds proves that Jacob Crook senior built, or re-built, two houses on our site - a cottage and a *"dwelling house"*- and completed the work by August 1817. In that month he borrowed £300 as a mortgage, but only after construction, rather than before building work started.

The 1872 document, called an Abstract of the Title, states that Crook had: *"since the purchase by him...erected on the piece or parcel of land first thereinbefore mentioned and described a messe or cottage and on the piece or parcel of land secondly thereinbefore described a messe or dwelling house"*.

In his will, after he died on 6 November 1819, Jacob Crook left everything, including our property, to his wife Mary. It was all to be looked after on her behalf by Thomas Thomas, a local pub landlord, and family member Thomas Crook, who ran a men's clothing shop. However, this pair renounced their role as executors and handed responsibility for carrying out the will to a lawyer, Richard Baylis.

The will stated that, on Mary's death, the estate would go in equal half shares to Jacob Crook's son, also called Jacob, and daughter Hannah, who were twins. Hannah was married to a plumber and glazier called Thomas Stroud.[30]

One can imagine Crook senior asking this handy son-in-law, Thomas Stroud, to cut and fit the window glass in his newly-completed house. And while he's at it, why not also get him to put in the drains and sewage system? It's even tempting to blame Stroud for a legacy of rather dodgy plumbing that still affects 60 Fairfield Road to this day!

WILLIAM HARRISON - CROOKED DEALS

As mentioned above, in 1826 Jacob Crook junior contracted to sell his half share in the property to William Harrison (for £150), ignoring the fact that, legally, it didn't belong to him until his mother Mary died. In fact, she lived on until 1841.[31] Harrison resided in the newer part of the premises from 1827 to 1828 or 1829, when he was declared bankrupt.

Every year, from 1820 to 1830, Harrison was listed in the annual Mathews' Bristol Directory as a *"leather factor"*, or merchant, trading at 58 or 59 Baldwin Street and Back Hall in the city centre. In each of those last two years, his profession was also given as *"glue manufacturer"* at Baptist Mills, (where St Werburghs meets the M32 today.) The now bankrupt William Harrison then disappeared from the records.

Jacob Crook junior, by contrast, seems to have prospered greatly, despite his suspect deal with Harrison. For several years from 1820, he was described in Mathews' Directory as a *"common brewer"*, of 6 Narrow Wine Street (his father's old address). In other words, he sold beer directly to the pubs, as his father had done.

Then from 1824, at the age of 28, in the same directory young Jacob suddenly became a *"gent"*, with no trade mentioned and living in the upmarket Brandon Cottage on Brandon Hill, Clifton. This was to remain his home for the next couple of decades.

After his bankruptcy in 1829, William Harrison's illegal half ownership of the Montpelier property was sold at auction to his major creditor. In another highly dubious transaction, it was later sold back to Jacob Crook junior.

Eventually, in 1842, Jacob would become sole owner when his sister Hannah sold her half share to him, following their mother's death.[32]

Hannah and Thomas Stroud had, in the 1830s, and maybe earlier, been living in what by now was called "Spring Cottage" (the original cottage). We can deduce this from our deeds, but they're mostly vague about dates. Before the first Census in 1841, it's much harder to pinpoint where families lived and for how long. Hannah and Thomas had seven children. Birth records show that six of them were born in Narrow Wine Street, where generations of Crooks

Brandon Cottage was Jacob Crook junior's home for about 25 years. (Photo: Paul Bullivant)

and Strouds had lived and traded as neighbours, brewers and plumbers/glaziers. Two of the couple's sons, Thomas and John, were twins, but the latter died in infancy.

Twins certainly ran in the Crook family in a big way. Jacob Crook junior's wife Sarah also gave birth to twins, both boys and named Henry and Alfred, in 1826. They already had a son, yet another Jacob, born in 1821. It may have been partly starting their own family that motivated the couple to sell up and move to somewhere bigger.

This begs the question: how did Jacob Crook junior get rich so quickly? A clue may lie in a much later Census, that of 1851, which described his occupation as *"Landed Property"*. The Napoleonic Wars had left the country with land prices and rents at rock bottom. It gave Crook an opportunity to buy and sell properties around Bristol at a handsome profit, as the market started to recover.

THE STORY SO FAR

The earliest origins of 60 Fairfield Road remain obscure. However, from the research, first by historian Mary Wright and then by ourselves, a clearer picture has emerged of the set-up soon after building work was completed by Jacob Crook senior, in 1817 or before.

The first residents of the cottage after Shurmer Bath and Jacob himself - if either man really did live there during construction - were probably Hannah and Thomas Stroud and their young children. First to inhabit the adjoining new house were, most likely, Hannah's twin brother, Jacob Crook junior, his wife Sarah and their first child.

This symmetrical arrangement was, it seems, what Jacob Crook senior had planned all along to house the next generation of his family. He wanted his twin son and daughter living in adjoining houses with their own families, both of them due eventually to inherit the property.

However, Jacob Crook's death, at the age of 50, in 1819 really upset the applecart. The brewer had left his entire estate to his wife, Mary, for it to be divided equally between their grown-up twins after Mary died. But Jacob junior ignored his father's will and agreed the sale of his share in the premises to William Harrison, although it belonged to his mother.

The result was a legal tangle which took many years to sort out. However, it also opened the door to the many and varied tenants who've helped give 60 Fairfield Road such a fascinating history.

RESEARCHING THE PEOPLE WHO LIVED IN YOUR HOUSE - EARLY NINETEENTH CENTURY

Things become a little easier to research after the turn of the nineteenth century, when more records were kept and more of them survive today. As towns and cities rapidly grew in population, civic organisations needed better administration. A bureaucracy developed to deal with the more complex social and economic landscape. The first Census was in 1801, but it was purely statistical and personal details weren't included until the Census of 1841. However, **births, deaths, marriages and baptisms** were all recorded by religious and civic organisations. They're often a good place to start, as long as you have at least a name and approximate date for one of your house occupants. The easiest route is via **genealogy websites,** referred to at the end of Chapter 1. They all have links to these records.

Sources from Bristol Archives and other archive collections:

1. **Title Deeds**. Bristol Archives holds large numbers of deeds for properties in the city and beyond, dating from the twelfth century. You may find old deeds in local Archives elsewhere, too, but more recent ones are less likely to be kept there. The deeds include conveyances, mortgages and leases. Each deed records changes in ownership, describes the property and any changes made to it and of course, most usefully, names the owners and occupiers. An 'abstract of title' summarises the deeds and is often easier to read than going through each hand written document. There are books and pamphlets, for example *Reading Old Title Deeds* by Julian Cornwall (1993), which could help you here. The reference to a "ruinous cottage" in the deeds for this house had been a tantalising clue to its history long before detailed research began.

2. **Trade and Street Directories.** These were like phone directories or Yellow Pages in the nineteenth and early twentieth centuries. Bristol Archives has trade directories from the 1760s onwards. The city's Central

Library also holds them for public viewing. But trade directories really came into their own in the 1800s. The earlier ones are arranged by alphabetical name, but later ones by street address, too. They often give the trade of the head of household and are a wonderful source of information about his or her occupation. Mathews' Bristol Directory, published annually, revealed Jacob Crook junior's meteoric rise in status and income in the 1820s.

3. **Taxes and Rates records.** Many types of rates and taxes were levied in British towns and cities in the nineteenth century. (See notes at the end of Chapter 1.) Records held by Bristol Archives are often just for the old city centre, but the Poor Rate books from the late 1700s and early 1800s that are available often cover a wider area. The Poor Rate was a tax collected from householders by parishes to provide for the poor. These records weren't explored for this book, but offer another avenue of research in many towns and cities.

4. **Property sale records.** Sale particulars, surveys and valuations of some notable houses and estates, together with plans and site maps, are available in Bristol Archives.

5. **Wills and inventories** of individuals and property. Bristol Archives keeps wills proved in Bristol (the process of probate managed by church courts), from 1546 to 1858. For example, Jacob Crook's will was found among them. Wealthier people's wills were proved elsewhere, at the Prerogative Court of Canterbury, and these records are held by the National Archives. These documents can provide details of an individual's wealth, assets and family relationships.

6. **Land owners' records.** These were often complex by the early 1800s, as entrepreneurship and rapid development encouraged landowners to cash in through buying and selling, like Jacob Crook junior. Records of the largest owners may be found in your local public Archives. In Bristol they hold, for example, those of the Society of Merchant Venturers, a powerful and very influential local organisation which owned a lot of property. The city corporations (later city councils), churches and charities, as well as

families and individuals, also owned land and property, again to be found in records at your local Archives.

Other sources for this chapter were **books** like Mary Wright's *Montpelier* and Latimer's *Annals of Bristol*. (The latter can be read online.) Local history books for your own area, as mentioned in Chapter 1, will provide useful background information. Wider-ranging history books and other texts may also aid your research.

CHAPTER 3

MID NINETEENTH CENTURY

THE MISSES PHIPPEN

One of the earliest tenants in our property, at first with William Harrison as her next door neighbour in the adjoining part, was a Miss Phippen. Land tax records for 1827 show a woman of that name living in a house owned by J. Crook, with Harrison also the resident of a house belonging to Crook. However, these records make no distinction between the two dwellings[33] on our site.

The house deeds also refer to both a Miss Phippen and Harrison as tenants, but don't specify when, or which of them lived in the cottage and which in the extension.

Every year, from 1826 to 1832, Mathews' annual Bristol directories included in their listings *"Phippen Misses Ladies' Boarding School Montpelier"*, without specifying its location. The address given in the 1833 directory changed to *"Ashley Hill"*, then again to *"Above the Asylum, Ashley Hill"* from 1834 to 1838.

The "Asylum", a short walk from Spring Cottage, was another name for the Blue Maids Orphanage for girls, which had opened in 1795. It was moved into a brand new building, slightly higher up Ashley Hill, in 1829.[34]

The boarding school was a separate establishment, either next door to the new orphanage building or a little further still up Ashley Hill, run by sisters Mary and Charlotte Phippen. Their father, Thomas Phippen, was an accountant and yet another Bristol Quaker. He had been appointed as local agent for the Coalbrookdale Company of Ironbridge in Shropshire, the country's original industrial heartland.

Thomas Phippen symbolised the close financial and business links between

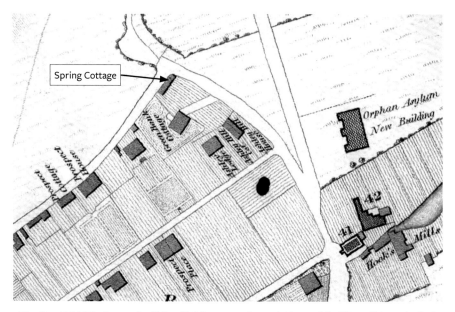

The Blue Maids' Orphanage for Girls, which became a close neighbour of the Misses Phippen Ladies' Boarding School, is marked "Orphan Asylum" on the Ashmead 1828 map (large new building on the right). Its previous site is marked 42. From the school and orphanage it was just a short walk to Spring Cottage. (Know Your Place/Bristol Archives 04481)

Bristol and the Shropshire iron industry, often involving influential Quakers. For the past century, merchants in Bristol had provided much of the capital for its development. This led to the emergence of numerous local city banks, and of a trade route for iron products from Shropshire, down the River Severn to Bristol and through the port.[35] Transportation had recently become easier with the opening of the Gloucester and Berkeley Canal (later named Gloucester and Sharpness Canal) in 1827.

In 1836 Thomas Phippen's Bristol office was in Castle Street, in the city centre, and his home just outside Montpelier, at 32 Wilson Street, St Pauls.[36] A year later, Thomas married for the second time when he and his new wife, also Mary, were both in their mid sixties.

Which of the Misses Phippen lived on the Spring Cottage site, or whether even both of Thomas's daughters did so, isn't clear. Their first names were always omitted in the relevant documentation. However, it seems at least one of them resided there from 1827 to about 1833.[37]

We can't be sure, either, of the boarding school's exact location. It had been going for about three years before the new orphanage building opened.

LADIES' BOARDING-SCHOOL,
ASHLEY HILL, near BRISTOL.
THE Misses PHIPPEN take this opportunity of thank-
ing their Friends for past favors, trusting still to merit their
patronage and support by continued attention to the health, comfort, and improvement of their Pupils; respectfully reminding
them, and the Public, that the Establishment will re-open July
the 8th, at the above-mentioned healthy and pleasant situation.
    N. B. There will be three or four Vacancies at the close of the
present recess.

Bristol Mercury, 29 June 1833

In that early period, when the address in Montpelier was left non-specific in the trade directories, it's even just possible the Phippen sisters used Spring Cottage as their school.

Plenty is known about the Blue Maids Orphanage, which owed its name to the colour of the girls' uniform. It was funded by generous local patrons, with about 60 residential places for orphaned girls from poor families. They were trained largely to become domestic servants in respectable local households.[38] However, we have scant information about the ladies' boarding school, and none at all about its relationship with the orphanage.

An advertisement (see above) placed by the Misses Phippen, though, in the *Bristol Mercury* newspaper on 29 June 1833, does reveal that the school's financial backers were Quakers, also known as "Friends", like their father Thomas. So, the Phippen school curriculum was based as much on instilling moral values and behaviour into the children as learning the 'three Rs'.

In 1835 the older Phippen sister, Mary, had reached the age of 40 when she decided to marry. Her husband was George Harding, a widower who ran a tailoring business at 24 Broad Street in central Bristol. Mary and Charlotte carried on with their school "above the Asylum" for another three years. Then Charlotte, who was eight years younger than her sister, left the city to set up her own ladies' boarding school at Newport in South Wales.

For the next decade, Charlotte Phippen lived with her pupils at the school on one of Newport's busiest newly-built streets, Commercial Road. The Wales Census of 1841 recorded nine girls boarding there, aged between five and 15, but no other live-in teachers apart from Charlotte.

Newport was a rapidly expanding industrial town, but with high levels of poverty.[39] Charlotte's pupils came from destitute local families, many of them orphaned through sickness and deprivation.

Newport was hit by a serious outbreak of cholera in 1849, which killed over 200 people in the town and hundreds more in the South Wales Valleys. However, Charlotte Phippen narrowly escaped it. She had returned to Bristol the previous year to run another school for "young ladies". This time it was at a house in Stokes Croft called Hope Villa, which also became her new home. Charlotte made this appeal to her Quaker patrons in Wales, via an announcement in the *Monmouthshire Merlin* local paper, on 8 January 1848:

MISS PHIPPEN,

IN announcing to her Friends in Newport and its vicinity, the removal of her Establishment, for the education of young Ladies, to Hope Villa, Catherine Place, Stoke's Croft, Bristol, begs gratefully to acknowledge the very liberal patronage and support she enjoyed during her residence amongst them, and hopes for a continuance of the same in her new residence.

Hope Villa is very salubriously situated; and Mis Phippen's attention will be untiringly devoted, as heretofore, to the mental and moral improvement of her pupils.

The school will re-open on the 12th instant.
Hope Villa, Bristol, January 3rd, 1848.

Monmouthshire Merlin, 8 January 1848

This notice sheds more light on the ethos of the Phippen educational establishments, which must also have applied to their original school in Montpelier. Essentially, they were small charity schools for daughters of the poor, subsidised by local Quaker benefactors. Charlotte relied on *"very liberal patronage and support"* to deliver *"the mental and moral improvement of her pupils"* in her own home. It's likely she had only a limited number of girls in her care.

Amazingly, Charlotte's pupils in Wales accompanied her to Bristol. The Census of 1851 found Charlotte living in the school at Hope Villa, Catherine Place, Stokes Croft, with three sisters from an Irish family in Newport. Their mother, Ann Barnes, had brought them up as a single parent in George Street, a central area of Newport full of dirty and insanitary slum housing. According to the 1841 Census, the Barnes household had then also included three other

This postcard, from the very early 1900s, shows Ashley Hill at its junction with Old Ashley Hill (on the left.) Spring Cottage stood just around the corner behind the horse and cart, but tantalisingly out of sight. The Blue Maids' Orphanage and, in the 1830s, the Misses Phippen Ladies' Boarding School, lay behind the wall and railings on the right. (Bristol Archives 43207/9/21/83)

children, but we can find no record of these or their mother after that year.

It seems the three remaining Barnes sisters, who would become pupils at Charlotte's boarding school in Newport, joined her when she went back to Bristol. The sisters had no one else to teach or look after them. They were: 18-year-old Susan Barnes, Matilda (aged 11) and Ann (9). Now, thanks to Charlotte's devoted philanthropy, the trio could continue their education and begin a new life in England.

Through later Censuses, we know that Charlotte Phippen went on to run girls' schools in Bristol for many more years. She took charge of two other establishments, in Stokes Croft and neighbouring St Pauls, always having at least a couple of pupils living with her. After Mary's husband George died, the Phippen sisters shared a home together at Charlotte's last school premises (28 Bishop Street, St Pauls) into old age. Both lived into their eighties, with Charlotte following Mary to the grave in 1887.

The Misses Phippen, especially Charlotte, were trailblazers for the major improvements in public education for both girls and boys that were to follow in the Victorian era. There are definite parallels between Charlotte Phippen

Hand-coloured photo of Mary Carpenter from about 1860. (Image: courtesy of Bristol Culture, Bristol Museum and Art Gallery).

and the great educational reformer Mary Carpenter, who also lived and worked in Bristol for most of her life.

Mary Carpenter (1807-1877) was of a similar age to Charlotte Phippen (1803-1887). As a young woman, Mary joined her mother in running the Mrs Carpenter Ladies' Boarding School in Great George Street, Brandon Hill. It had been set up by her father, who was a Unitarian minister in Lewins Mead next to Stokes Croft. This was in the late 1820s, at about the same time as the Misses Phippen, daughters of a Quaker industrialist, launched their school in Montpelier.[40] We don't know if the Phippens ever met the Carpenters, but it's quite possible they did.

While Charlotte was running her next schools, in Newport and then back in Bristol, for impoverished girls, Mary Carpenter started a "ragged" school in Lewins Mead, to provide education, food and clothing for children from destitute families. She also set up a reformatory school for delinquent boys in Kingswood, and another for girls at the Red Lodge in the 1850s.

Mary Carpenter is still deservedly a famous name, whereas Charlotte and Mary Phippen are entirely forgotten. There's a Phippen Street in Bristol (in the Redcliffe area), but it was named after Robert Phippen, a lawyer who became the city's Mayor in 1840.

SUMMER HOUSE

Our Spring Cottage title deeds outline an indenture, or agreement, of 1 July 1833. It states that *"there had been erected and built upon the site of the summer house and the piece or parcel of ground first therebefore mentioned or on some part thereof a tenement or dwelling house which was then in the occupation of Thomas*

Spring Cottage from the rear – was it an eighteenth century "summer house"?

Stroud plumber".

The document continues: *"There had been erected and built upon the second piece or parcel of meadow pasture or arable land adjoining to Hooks Mill Lane [Old Ashley Hill] or on some part thereof a tenement or dwelling house which was then in the possession of William Beaumont teacher of languages."*

As well as now describing the cottage as being on the site of a *"summer house"*, this extract is highly significant in that it refers to two houses and two separate households on the premises. They were clearly planned and built as such by Jacob Crook.

It also identifies the families living in each house on that specific day, 1 July 1833, to give us a fascinating snapshot in time. They were: Crook's daughter Hannah and her husband Thomas (the Strouds) in the cottage, and tenant William Beaumont in the adjoining newer house. Both families had a multitude of children, so they were two packed households.

The reference in our deeds to an earlier *"summer house"* also suggests this could be the *"ruinous cottage"* that stood here in 1812. Roger Leech, in his book *The Town House in Medieval and Early Modern Bristol*, relates how it was popular among the city's prosperous business community, in the seventeenth and eighteenth centuries, to build themselves second homes on the edge of Bristol.[41]

Known as garden houses or summer houses, they were intended mainly for leisure and recreational use, as an escape from the dirt, noxious smells and pestilence of the city. Perhaps it was a cottage for this purpose that Shurmer Bath had in mind, or already existed, when he started work on our site.

Shurmer may have been inspired by the example of his friend Richard Champion, the porcelain manufacturer and brother of the diarist Sarah Fox.

Richard kept a summer residence in Henbury, just outside Bristol on the north-west side. In the introduction to her modern edition of Sarah's diary, Madge Dresser makes the following observation:

"*A number of the wealthier Quakers seem to have acquired country residences near the city around this time: the Reeves, the Wrights and the Harfords, to name a few. They attempted with other well-heeled Dissenters to live a more 'genteel' and polite lifestyle, but on their own terms.*" [42]

It's not known when one house was 'knocked through' to the other on the Spring Cottage site and connecting doorways put in. However, mostly they seem to have remained separate households until well into the twentieth century.

This is reflected in some anomalies in street numbering on Fairfield Road over the years. Our address has been given either as numbers 58 and 60, or just 60, or 56, or even 50 at one time. Nowadays, 58 Fairfield Road has disappeared completely as an address. The next house along the street from us at 60 is number 56.

WILLIAM BEAUMONT - FRENCH CONNECTION

There's evidence that William Beaumont lived as a tenant in the newer construction adjoining the cottage from 1833 – or perhaps earlier - to 1835 or 1836. As described previously, our deeds refer to him being Thomas and Hannah Stroud's next door neighbour on the premises in July 1833. Beaumont's name also appeared in the 1835 Bristol Poll Book (register of voters), where he was listed as a *"French teacher"* living in *"Up. Montpelier"*.

However, the first recorded mention we've found of William Beaumont in Bristol came earlier, in the Mathews' Trade Directory for 1828. He was listed as *"Hamiltonian Professor of Languages"* at 44 College Street, near Bristol Cathedral.

This grand title derived from a controversial new method of teaching languages, started by an Irishman, James Hamilton, in the United States and brought over to Britain. Based on word-for-word translation rather than grammar, the so-called Hamiltonian system was popular at the time for fast learning. It was, however, dismissed as fraudulent by some in America and on this side of the Atlantic.[43]

William married a local woman, Sarah Turnbull, in Bristol in 1822, and the couple had seven children between 1826 and 1836. Two of them, Florence and Alfred, were probably born while the family was living in the newer, and larger, house on our site in Montpelier. They already had four children when they moved in. It would have been a crowded household, with money extremely tight.

However, William Beaumont wasn't what he seemed and had a secret identity – as a French nobleman. His real name was *Guillaume de Beaumont*. His

William (Guillaume) Beaumont in later life
(Photo: courtesy of Francis Wright)

aristocratic parents, and perhaps the rest of his family, were executed by guillotine during the terrible aftermath of the French Revolution in 1789.

The infant *Guillaume* was imprisoned at first, but then escaped, with the help of loyal servants, when about five years old. He was smuggled out of France to England and eventually ended up in Bristol, as a language teacher, husband and father.[44]

Guillaume, no doubt, became "William" to disguise his origins at a time when, soon after Waterloo, being French was about as popular as being German at the end of the First World War.

An article in the *Biggleswade Chronicle*, on 13 July 1923, reveals more about William's French ancestry. This was written long after his death, in reference to the marriage of his granddaughter in London. It tells us that William had a French title, *Guillaume de Beaumont et Maine*, which he renounced following his escape to England.

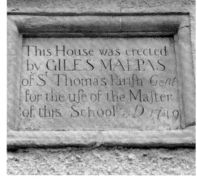

Chatterton House, formerly the Free School Master's residence, where William Beaumont allegedly provoked an axe attack on him by his young female servant.

VIOLENT OUTRAGE

Despite his secrets, "Professor" Beaumont became a teacher at the Pyle Street (later Pile Street) Free School in Redcliffe. This was a charity school for boys, whose Master in the mid eighteenth century had been the poet Thomas Chatterton's father, and where Chatterton himself was once a pupil.[45]

By 1831 Beaumont had been appointed as Master of the school himself. It entitled him to a house next door to it, purpose-built 80 years earlier for any man holding that position to live in. The school and street have long since been demolished. However, Chatterton House, as it's now known, where the poet was born, is still standing.

That summer of 1831, not long before moving to Montpelier, Beaumont was allegedly attacked with an axe in the Master's house by his 17-year-old female servant, Mary Tamplin. According to a report of the court case in a London newspaper, the *Morning Post*, on 4 January 1832, Tamplin was *"charged with maliciously cutting and wounding her master with the intent to murder him"*.

More details had earlier been given by the *Bristol Mercury* on 26 July 1831, under the headline *"Violent Outrage"*. The city's magistrates took a statement on oath from Beaumont, giving his side of what happened:

"He states that he awoke from his sleep about six o'clock in the morning, in consequence of having received several wounds in the head, inflicted by the prisoner with a hatchet, and on looking up he saw her standing over him with the weapon in her hands; that he struggled with her, and on getting out of bed alarmed his wife,

who slept in another room and who came to his assistance, and that he had given the prisoner no provocation whatever for such conduct. Mrs Beaumont stated that on hearing the noise she got up, and saw the prisoner and her husband on the landing place, and the blood flowing from the wounds he had received in his head."

Mary Tamplin then made her own statement to the court, which gave a very different account of the circumstances. The young servant accused Beaumont of having provoked the attack by trying to rape her:

"After consulting with her mother, who was called in at this part of the proceedings, the prisoner said she went upstairs to call her master, as she usually did, when he caught hold of her and held her on the bed, and used her in a very unbecoming manner; and in taking hold of her he tore her skirt; she told him if he did not let her alone she would get something and strike him; after he had kept her on the bed for about two minutes she got away and went down stairs, but being obliged to go up again she took the hatchet in her hand; she did not say anything to him then, but he caught hold of her two or three times, when she struck him with the hatchet; he had struck her two or three times."

The *Bristol Mercury* reported that Mary Tamplin was committed for trial at the next Assizes. However, it seems the trial never took place.

RIOTING IN THE STREETS

Three months later, while Mary was still held in custody, the 1831 Bristol Riots broke out. It was a spontaneous uprising in protest at the blocking of electoral reform in Parliament by a reactionary establishment, which included the hero of Waterloo, the Duke of Wellington.

In late October many public buildings and private houses were looted and demolished, or set on fire. Some of the rioters released Mary Tamplin, and all the other prisoners, from the city's jail. After three days of mayhem, soldiers with drawn swords eventually charged the mob in Queen Square.

Official estimates put the number killed in the brutal suppression at about 12, but hundreds more rioters are thought to have died in the burning buildings. In her book *Perilous Question: the Drama of the Great Reform Bill 1832*, Antonia Fraser gives a staggeringly high figure for the death toll. She asserts that probably as many as 400 lost their lives, many of them burnt to death in a

'Charge of the 3rd Dragoon Guards in Queen Square', watercolour drawing by William James Muller with Thomas Leeson Rowbotham. (Image: courtesy of Bristol Culture, Bristol Museum & Art Gallery.)

drunken state after helping themselves to large quantities of liquor in people's houses.[46]

In the following New Year, a Special Commission, led by the Lord Chief Justice and with a Grand Jury, began to hear evidence on alleged crimes committed during the riots. They also reviewed cases involving prisoners already in custody at the time of the riots, who would have been tried before had it not been for the disturbances.

First on that list was Mary Tamplin. According to a *Bristol Mirror* report on 7 January 1832, the Lord Chief Justice advised the Commission that, before Tamplin's trial went ahead, William Beaumont should be *"interrogated very strictly and closely"* as to what had given rise to the attack by his servant .

On 19 January, the *Bath Chronicle and Weekly Gazette* reported on the sentencing of the rioters, which included four hangings and seven men transported overseas. The writer added this update on the Tamplin case:

"It is understood there are very peculiar circumstances connected with the affair. In consequence of application made on the affidavit of the police surgeon that the prisoner was labouring under inflammatory fever, and could not, without

endangering her life appear in court, her trial was yesterday postponed.”

We can find no further reference to Mary Tamplin in the newspaper archives. It appears the prosecution was quietly dropped, to avoid shaming a man in a position of authority at a time when anarchy threatened. Perhaps it was no coincidence that William Beaumont then moved his family out to the quiet suburbs, and resurfaced living in Montpelier.

GUILLAUME DE MONTPELIER

While Beaumont and family resided in the newer section of our premises, he ran his own languages academy at 23 Bridge Street, by Bristol Bridge. (This street was later destroyed in a bombing raid during the Second World War.) In the Mathews’ Directory of 1836, Beaumont was described as a *“Teacher of the French, Italian, Latin and Spanish Languages”* at the academy.

Learning continental languages was much in demand at the time. This was especially so in a prosperous trading city and major port, with plenty of fashionable young gentlemen organising their ‘Grand Tour’ in southern Europe. Foreign travel had been halted by the Napoleonic Wars, but was now making a comeback.

However, it wasn’t all plain sailing. In November 1835 the *London Gazette* recorded William Beaumont, *“late of Montpelier and keeping a school at 23 Bridge Street”*, being taken to court in Bristol for an insolvency hearing. Beaumont may have avoided bankruptcy, though, since he and his academy were listed once again in Mathews’ Directory the following year.

In 1837, however, that directory made no mention of the academy in Bridge Street, although Beaumont was still described as a *“Professor of Languages”*. He was now in charge of another teaching establishment, the Grove House Academy at 34 Queen Square, and remained so for the next two years. By now, German had bcen added as a fifth language in his repertoire, plus other academic subjects. Yet in the Mathews listings for 1840, William Beaumont’s name had gone.

Wlliam Beaumont left Bristol for Liverpool, where the 1841 Census found him living in the Everton district. In 1846, now back to using his real name *Guillaume*, he again faced bankruptcy proceedings. The same happened to him

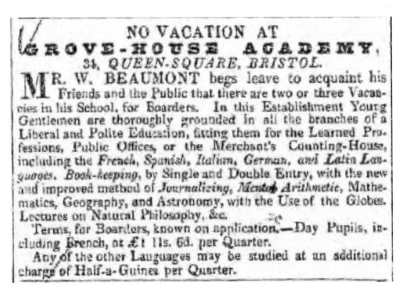

This advertisement was published in the Bristol Mercury on 22 June 1839 for William Beaumont's Grove House Academy at 34 Queen Square.

for a third time in 1852, when he was a *"schoolmaster"* in nearby Southport in Lancashire.[47]

Beaumont had, for some years, been Principal of Heaton Mount, a select boarding school in the town for a maximum of just 12 pupils. He had appointed his own eldest son, the Rev Henry Beaumont, as Vice Principal, aged just 24. Henry was also a local curate in Southport.

In the 1851 Census, Beaumont's wife and all four of their daughters - Sarah (22), Clara (20), Florence (18) and Estelle (14) - were living at the school with him, also a tutor and three servants. In total, Beaumont's residential staff and family equalled the number of pupils. He also hired *"Visiting Masters from Liverpool"*. No wonder he kept on running out of money!

Despite his financial troubles, an upbeat advertisement for the school appeared in the *Leeds Mercury* on 27 March 1852:

"The Principal of Heaton Mount Select School, Southport, Lancashire begs to direct the attention of parents to the singular purity and salubrity of the sea air of Southport, which is almost invariably the means of restoring health and strength to the delicate and weakly. His establishment offers unusual advantages for the education of young gentlemen in every way; it is conducted upon Christian principles; the modern languages are taught, without extra charge; and the treatment ensures

the comforts of home."

By 1861 Beaumont had retired - to another seaside town. The Census of that year gave William/ *Guillaume* Beaumont's address, with his wife, Sarah, as a boarding house in Worthing, on the Sussex coast. He died that year, in his late sixties. However, Sarah outlived him by more than 20 years until her own death in 1887, at the age of 86.

The Rev Henry Beaumont, William/Guillaume's eldest son, was Vice Principal of Heaton Mount School when only 24. Later in life, he became a clergyman in Brighton. (Photo: courtesy of Francis Wright)

GENTLEMAN'S SON IN THE WORKHOUSE

Meanwhile, back in Bristol, the Census of 1841 tells us that by then William Beaumont's former neighbour on the Spring Cottage site, Hannah Stroud, had moved back to Narrow Wine Street in the city centre. This was the Crook family's old home neighbourhood, where Hannah's father and brother had traded as brewers and the Strouds were still plumbing.

One assumes that Hannah's husband Thomas had now retired, or was incapable of working, as the Census gave her occupation as plumber in his place. She had most likely taken over the family business temporarily. Their two surviving sons, Thomas (now 20) and John (15), would both become plumbers/glaziers, but perhaps neither was quite old or experienced enough yet to be put in charge. Thomas Stroud senior died in 1847, aged 61.

Our house deeds mention someone called William Watson as a tenant of the newer dwelling after William Beaumont. This is corroborated by the 1841 Census, which listed a whole family of Watsons on the premises. They were: 50-year-old William Penrose Watson, a man of *"independent means"* born in Ireland; his much younger wife Ellen, aged 30; and their three children - another

Chandos Villa, Cotham, where Jacob Crook junior lived in the early 1850s. *(Photo: Paul Bullivant)*

William P. (12), John Thomas (8), and Sylla (4). The couple had married in Bristol in 1840, so it seems all their children were born out of wedlock.

We found no more information about the family until, on 29 November 1848, the death was recorded of William Penrose Watson at his home, now in the Bedminster area of Bristol. His death certificate, which described him as a *"gentleman"*, said the cause was *"complete exhaustion apparently the effect of great mental depression"*. William's namesake eldest son, then aged 19, was with him when he died.[48]

What happened afterwards to his widow Ella and daughter Sylla isn't known. Nor can we be certain about the Watson sons. Identifying the younger one, John, from official records, and then tracing his life history, has been like trying to make a complicated jigsaw with only a few of the pieces. However, there's a trail of circumstantial evidence to be drawn from five Censuses over a 50-year-period.

A man called John Watson, of the right age (28), was listed in the 1861 Census as a married man, born in Bristol, and now living as a *"lodger"* with two other families (but not his wife), at Camberwell in London. He was employed as a *"floor cloth trowler"*.

The Census of 1871 found a John Watson, now aged 38, back in Bristol with his own family and with his occupation given as *"chair carver"*. He shared accommodation in the St Paul's area with his wife Elizabeth, their three young children and another married couple, who were listed as *"visitors"* and both [house] *"painters"*.

In 1881 the next Census referred to a 48-year old John Watson, born in Bristol, (again the right age and birthplace), who had now moved to Birmingham and was a *"boarder"* with a married couple in Great Russell Street. He was now working as a *"floor cloth maker"* (the same trade as 20 years earlier in London).

In 1901 a widower of the same name, born in Bristol and now 68, had fallen on hard times. He was an *"inmate"* at the Birmingham Workhouse. His trade was now given in the Census as *"painter"*. In 1911 John Watson was still living in the same workhouse, at the age of 77, and again described as a *"house painter"*. The Bristolian with an Irish family background had finally been put in a separate wing, provided for the oldest inmates who were of good character. He died two years later, in 1913.

By the end of the nineteenth century, there were still hundreds of crowded workhouses across Britain, where destitute men and women were given meagre food and a roof over their heads, in return for hard labour.[49] However, conditions had gradually improved, for the elderly and infirm in particular. So, John Watson's final years may have been a little less grim than the earlier image portrayed by Dickens in *Oliver Twist*.

The elder Watson son seems to have fared somewhat better than John. In 1851 a William P. Watson, aged 22, was living as a *"visitor"* at 60 College Street, near Bristol Cathedral, employed as a *"commissioning agent"*. That same year, William married Caroline Taylor in Clifton. But that is the last record we have of him until his death in Bristol in 1903, when he was about 76.

Returning to that first Census of 1841, it confirmed the address of the Watsons' landlord in Montpelier, Jacob Crook junior, as still being Brandon Cottage, Clifton. He had lived there, at the bottom of Brandon Hill, with his wife Sarah and their twin sons Henry and Alfred (now aged 15), since 1824.

According to various trade directory listings, Jacob was still at Brandon Cottage in 1849, now a widower. He then moved to Chandos Villa (now 128

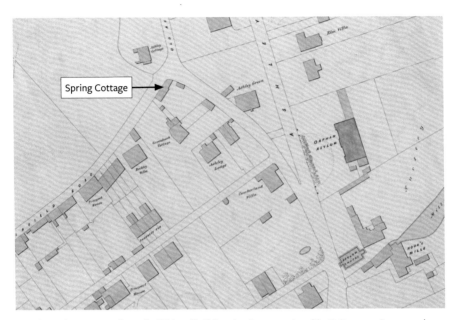

Ashmead's 1855 map showed additional building development since his 1828 survey. For example, there was a new terrace of four houses between Rockley Villa and Prospect House on Fairfield Road. Opposite Spring Cottage a new house, Ashley Cottage, had been built, whose name was changed later to Ashley Villa. (Know Your Place/Bristol Archives 40860/1)

Cotham Brow) in Cotham. In 1856 Jacob was living in Cornwall Cottage on Richmond Hill, Clifton. All were smart addresses, indicating the junior Crook had continued to do well as a property speculator - unlike poor Shurmer Bath before him.

RESEARCHING THE PEOPLE WHO LIVED IN YOUR HOUSE – MID NINETEENTH CENTURY

The first useable **Census** was carried out in 1841, then every ten years after that. It's searchable by name, date and place on both these genealogy websites, mentioned in previous chapters: https://ancestry.co.uk and https://findmypast.co.uk. Here, together with your **house deeds**, may be the best place to start researching who was living in your house in the mid nineteenth century.

Bristol's population, like that of many British industrial cities, grew rapidly after 1800, when it was around 70,000. By 1881 it had reached 266,000. The main reason was the rapid development of the port and its industries, bringing great wealth to Bristol. The prosperous middle classes were building houses further out from the dirty and smelly central area, where the working class tended to live. During the period covered in this chapter, from the late 1820s to about 1860, the availability of mass-produced **printed material** increased greatly, reflecting technological, economic and social change. All this has left more resources for the amateur house historian to draw on.

Among the most important are **newspapers**. By the 1820s Britain had hundreds of newspapers, nearly all local and now much better produced. In many cities, including Bristol, several were being published, often for varying readerships. They were the mass media of the time and offer a wealth of interesting material for the house researcher. Local news was obviously prominent, but the content also included family events (births, marriages, deaths) and business notices, letters, obituaries and advertisements. Any of these can reveal fascinating details about the lives of past residents in your house.

The **British Newspaper Archive** https://www.britishnewspaperarchive.co.uk/ contains digitised facsimiles of most newspapers published in Britain in the nineteenth century. Twentieth century newspapers are gradually being added. The archive is searchable by title, name, location, date or keyword. This is a subscription website, like the family history sites mentioned previously. Again, therefore, it's best to wait until you have specific names, places or stories to seek. However, you may be surprised at what you find by chance. One piece of information can lead you to another. This was the case in discovering the rather shady history of William Beaumont, revealed in this chapter through a series of dramatic newspaper articles.

Local Archives and reference libraries usually have original and/or digitised copies of newspapers from the 1800s. Bristol Central Reference Library, for example, holds late nineteenth century copies of all the local newspapers, plus special collections of earlier newspapers on particular topics.

If you discover, perhaps through a newspaper report, that any of your former house occupants had a criminal record, then **Court Records** for Central, County and Crown Courts can be searched online in various places. A good overview of where to look can be obtained at https://www.nationalarchives.gov.uk/help-with-your-research/research-guides/criminals-and-convicts/ You'll need to know where the trial took place and what kind of court tried the case, as there's no central name index of convicted criminals.

Other sources related to crime are:

1. **Criminal registers for England and Wales 1791-1892**, available via the Ancestry website.

2. **Records of criminals, convicts and prisoners 1770-1935,** found on the Findmypast website.

As mentioned earlier, both of the above are subscription sites.

Many people were unfortunate enough to fall into poverty during this period. You may find out that some of your past house occupants, and/or their children, ended up in a **Workhouse**. Under the Poor Law Amendment Act of 1834, parishes in England and Wales formed Poor Law Unions, each with its Union Workhouse financed by local taxes. Hundreds of new workhouses were built all over the country, to provide housing and basic food for those unable to support themselves. Conditions were intentionally very harsh as a deterrent to anyone capable of work. By the 1850s, most workhouses were filled with the old, the physically or mentally ill, unmarried mothers and orphans. Detailed and accurate records of inmates and staff were kept, and are available from various sources. However, in Bristol many workhouse records were destroyed by bombing in the Second World War.

The website https://findmypast.co.uk has links to workhouse records in Britain. General information, and a searchable database, are available on **The Workhouse** website http://www.workhouses.org.uk/.

Another resource already touched upon in the previous chapter guide is the **Trade Directory**. These had proliferated by the mid nineteenth century, and there were many different ones, each with its own focus and style. Your local reference library and/or Archives will have copies of these. In this chapter, Mathews' annual Bristol directories were especially useful for researching the Misses Phippen and their schools. Some local directories (or sections of them), for specific years, are available to read online, free of charge. These are usually editions from university or private collections.

By the mid 1800s, **maps and street plans** were of higher quality because British cities were being surveyed by more accurate techniques. In Bristol George Ashmead's 1828 map was the first detailed street map of the city. Old maps can be viewed in local Archives, reference libraries or museums. As mentioned before, the Know Your Place website http://www.kypwest.org.uk/ has many interactive digitised historical maps to explore. Most of the ones reproduced in this book came from this source.

Rural areas (not Montpelier) were covered by **tithe maps** and their related apportionment books. The maps show each plot of land, while the books describe them and identify the owner/occupier. These records are kept in local Archives. For country places near Bristol, the tithe maps are available on Know Your Place.

Bristol Archives holds a substantial collection of **building plans** for nineteenth and twentieth century houses. Similar records may also be kept in the local Archives of other areas.

CHAPTER 4

LATE NINETEENTH CENTURY

THE VINERS – TROUBLE BREWING

For much of the nineteenth and early twentieth centuries, Spring Cottage and adjoining house were inhabited not by the owners but by their tenants. Well-off local businessmen would buy the property as an investment to make money, rather than as a home for themselves.

There was nothing unusual about this for the time. It followed a common pattern across urban England. Since large families, sometimes with up to 10 children, were also the norm, it explains why so many houses were in multiple occupation.

The Census of 1851 recorded another brewing family, the Viners, living in *"Spring Cottage"*. It was one of the first official uses of that address. Originally from Berkshire, the family remained tenants for the next 30 years. The family's names were listed in the Census as: Alfred Viner, 66-year-old *"hop merchant"*; his second wife Elizabeth (65); and their daughter, also Elizabeth (aged 24 and unmarried.)

According to Hunt's Directory of 1849, Alfred ran a business as *"hop factor and dealer"* from 68 Old Market Street. Two of his sons, George and Henry Viner, had their own partnership of *"brewers"* and *"maltsters"* in Broad Plain. However, Hunt's Directory of 1850, and Mathews' Directory of the following year, both showed Alfred trading as a hop merchant from home at *"Spring Cottage Ashley Hill"*. Then, in May 1853, the *Bristol Mercury* reported his death there, at the age of 68.

Alfred Viner's switch to running his business at Spring Cottage may have been connected to severe financial trouble. In 1849, the year before that move from Old Market, he was declared bankrupt. A report of the court proceedings appeared in the *Bristol Times and Mirror* on 8 December.

This showed that Alfred had been struggling to pay off creditors and building up debts since the mid 1830s. He had *"commenced business without capital...kept no cash book and his accounts were generally of an unsatisfactory nature"*. Alfred was barred from trading for three months because of his *"mixed misfortune and recklessness"*.

It seems the bankrupt hop merchant was forced to shut down his business in Old Market, before re-opening it at home in Montpelier. Perhaps the huge stress all this must have caused for a man in his late sixties contributed to Alfred's death, just a couple of years later.

By 1861, even without Alfred, the number of Viners living together had increased. Confusingly, the Census called their home *"Spring Villa Old Ashley Hill"*. Alfred's widow Elizabeth, now aged 76, was still there, and her occupation had become *"interest in mortgages"*. She still had daughter Elizabeth living with her, now 34 and still unmarried.

Mother and daughter had been joined by three grown-up Viner sons, also born in Hungerford: George (44), described as a *"traveller for brewers"*, Frederick (39), and Edward (37). The latter two were both *"ironmonger's assistants"*. All three were unmarried, like Elizabeth.

George Viner was the same one who, a decade earlier, had been trading as a brewer and maltster in Broad Plain with another brother, Henry. In 1862 Frederick married in Belfast, but returned to Bristol. He then moved out of Spring Cottage soon afterwards to set up home with his new wife, just up the road at Ashley Down.

In the 1871 Census, our premises were listed for the first time as being in Fairfield Road. By then, Alfred Viner's widow Elizabeth had also died, at the age of 79, and so, too, had their son George. However, their youngest son Edward, now 47, was still living there, employed as a *"clerk"*. Their spinster daughter Elizabeth, also middle-aged, had become a *"housekeeper"* (presumably for Edward).

JOSEPH HUMPHREY - FARMER TO COAL MERCHANT

The Fairfield Road household of 1871 was further expanded by three lodgers. Someone (most likely a Viner) had previously advertised several times in the local newspapers, offering *"pleasant apartments"* or lodgings for a *"gentleman dining in the city"*. This was one such ad, placed in the *Bristol Times and Mirror* on 30 March 1870:

L ODGINGS and BOARD in a quiet family for a Gentleman dining in the city —Apply at Spring Cottage, Fairfield-road. 1c6

The lodgers who moved in were: James Robertson (24), born in Scotland and a *"telegraphist"*; Joseph Humphrey (57), born in Surrey and a *"clerk"*; and his 21-year-old son Harry, an *"insurance clerk"*. We have no information on how the accommodation was shared out between them and the Viners.

Father and son Joseph and Harry Humphrey had presumably left the South East to find work. They were an unusual pair, in that Joseph had previously been a farmer, with 200 acres of land at Mickleham in Surrey, and then a farm bailiff, living with his wife Martha and four children.

Why Joseph changed his profession so dramatically and moved to Bristol as an office clerk, with his son but without his wife and three daughters, is a mystery. He and Martha may have separated. However, in the 1881 Census, each was still shown as married, but with Joseph still lodging in Bristol, (no longer at Spring Cottage), and Martha living in Devon with one of their daughters.

In that Census Joseph Humphrey was described as a *"commission agent"*. Later, in the Census of 1891, he was a 77-year-old *"coal merchant"* lodging in Dove Street, Kingsdown. He died in Bristol, aged 82, in 1896. Martha Humphrey had died before him in 1890, at the age of 74, still in Devon and still married to Joseph, but apart.

Their son Harry moved up to County Durham when still a young man and became a clerk at Westoe Colliery. He married a woman from Newcastle called Hannah Scott. The couple eventually had seven children, and he spent the rest of his working life in the North-East and Yorkshire, remaining a colliery clerk.

It was quite a journey for a farmer's son, born in Dorking, and resident for a while in our house in Montpelier.

THE PLOT THICKENS

Jacob Crook junior still owned Spring Cottage when he died in 1872, a decade after his twin sister Hannah. He was 76 and, for 30 years, had made a very good living out of collecting rent from his tenants there and from other houses in Bristol. The Crook family then sold the whole Spring Cottage property by auction to Henry Lee, a local butcher, for £415.[50]

The auction was advertised in the *Western Daily Press* on 19 June 1872 (see below). It not only confirms that Edward Viner still remained there as a tenant, but also depicted the property as one integrated house, not two, called Spring Cottage:

> Lot 6.—All that MESSUAGE or Dwelling-house and Garden, situate in FAIRFIELD ROAD, MONTPELIER, and called SPRING COTTAGE, now in the occupation of Mr Edward Vinor, as yearly tenant.

The conveyance document in our deeds for the 1872 sale also portrayed it all as just one dwelling called Spring Cottage in Fairfield Road, as did the legal paperwork in subsequent changes of ownership until 1925.

However, in terms of who lived in the property, as opposed to who owned it, our story is about to become even more tangled. Over the next three decades, from 1872 until the turn of the twentieth century, a bewildering array of diverse tenants came and went, in large numbers worthy of a Dickens novel and with many dramas on the way.

Edward Viner, with his sister Elizabeth probably still housekeeping for him, continued to live on the Spring Cottage premises from 1873 until 1879. That was the residential address given for him by Wright's Directory every year during that period.

According to the next Census, in 1881 Spring Cottage was being rented by a 46-year-old woman called Georgina Davis. She had been widowed twice and her occupation was given as *"houses and dividends"*.

Her second husband, George Davis, had owned houses, so perhaps Georgina continued his business after he died in 1869, aged only 35. Her maiden name had been Matthews, and she was married only briefly to her first husband, William Winsborrow, who was a seaman and died of a fever at sea in 1855.

Georgina shared Spring Cottage with her 20-year-old son George, whose occupation was given in the 1881 Census as *"apprentice"*, and daughter Annie (18). It seems that Georgina had brought up both children alone, after losing her second husband 12 years earlier. The household was completed by a

16 Effingham Road in St Andrews, where a former Spring Cottage resident, Annie Vile, and husband Frederick were living with their 10 children in 1911. (Photo: Paul Bullivant)

"visitor" named John Box (49), who was a *"chemist (out of business)"*.

In March 1882, Georgina Davis must have decided that more help was needed around the house. An advertisement was posted in the *Western Daily Press*: *"WANTED, General Servant, aged 13 to 16. Good character. – Apply Spring Cottage, Fairfield Road, Ashley Hill."*

Her son and daughter, George and Annie, both married while the family was living in Spring Cottage. However, Georgina had only a short time left to share their happiness. On 5 January 1885, the *Western Daily Press* reported her death. She had passed away at home in Montpelier, at the age of 49, with the loss *"deeply regretted"* by family and friends.

Georgina Davis's daughter Annie and her husband, whose name was Frederick Vile, went on to have 10 children. In the 1911 Census, all 12 members of the Vile family were recorded as living together, half a mile away across St Andrews Park, at 16 Effingham Road.

After Georgina Davis's death and the departure of her married offspring, two branches of the same family, the Vowles, found themselves living almost

'A Maid Sweeping' by Henry Meynell Rheam (1859-1920) (Image: courtesy of Bonhams.)

opposite each other in Fairfield Road. In 1886, a 30-year-old travelling corn merchant, Walter Brown Vowles, was listed in Wright's Directory as residing in Spring Cottage. He had moved in as a tenant, together with his wife, Mary Ann, and sons, Harold (then aged 8) and Walter (4). A third son, Sydney, was probably born in the house.

At this point we also find a mysterious link between Walter Vowles' family and their immediate predecessors in Spring Cottage, the Davises. The maiden name of Walter's wife, Mary Ann, was Box. In 1886 the couple had living with them and their children Mary Ann's younger brother, 16-year-old Henry E. Box.

In fact, Mary Ann and Henry's father was John Box – the same *"chemist (out of business)"* who had been staying with Georgina Davis's family as a *"visitor"* in 1881. The Vowles and Box families clearly had close ties with the Davises, but we've been unable to establish how or why.

The Vowles family also had close relations in a house just across the street, known then as Ashley Villa and, before that in the mid 1800s, as Ashley Cottage. Heading that household was Walter's uncle, William Henry Vowles. He ran a brush manufacturing business from 5 Castle Street in the city centre. But every year, from 1873 to 1879, Wright's Directory also gave his residential address as Ashley Villa, Fairfield Road. William lived there with his wife Elizabeth, at least three of their five children, and his older sister Fanny.

William Vowles had gradually expanded his business in Castle Street, after setting it up as a young man. By the time of the 1871 Census, he was employing *"13 men and 3 boys"*. Brushes, brooms and mops were still an essential everyday item for any household, until well after the first powered vacuum cleaners appeared in the early 1900s.

In 1879 William Vowles died, at the early age of 48, but his wife Elizabeth then took over the firm and ran it for many years herself. The 1881 Census gave her occupation as a *"brush manufacturer"*, living in Ashley Villa with daughter Julia (24), and sons Edgar (19) and William (14). Elizabeth's sister-in-law Fanny was also still there with them. All five of her children, including her two eldest (and now married) sons Frederick (26) and Arthur (23), worked in the family business.

Elizabeth Vowles remained in Ashley Villa into old age, while opposite in Spring Cottage, according to Kelly's Directory, Walter Vowles' family were still tenants in 1889. However, by the time of the next Census in 1891, they had moved to 17 Berkeley Road in nearby Bishopston, taking young Henry Box with them.

Vowles was a common family name in Bristol. For example, Wright's Directory for 1886 had 34 entries under that name, listed by their trade and/or residential addresses in the city.

We don't know why Walter Vowles chose to live only a few steps away from his uncle William's house in Fairfield Road. However, by the time he moved in, William had already died. By then, also, William's widow Elizabeth was in charge of their brush making firm, as well as their household. She would have needed all the family help she could get to cope. Having the much younger nephew Walter, and Mary Ann, living so close by in Spring Cottage no doubt made a big difference.

W.H. Vowles and Sons continued as a thriving family business in the centre of Bristol until the mid twentieth century. The firm's Eagle Brushworks in Broad Weir survived the Second World War bombing, but was later demolished for redevelopment. In the early 1900s, William and Elizabeth Vowles' son Arthur opened a second brush factory, this time at Stonehouse in Gloucestershire. During the 1930s the firm employed over 160 workers.

A TURBULENT MARRIAGE

Although Spring Cottage was declared empty in the 1891 Census, Wright's Directory for that year named a John B. McLaine as living there for what must have been just a few months. McLaine (or McLean), a Scottish builder and

ASSAULT ON A FATHER-IN-LAW AT NEWPORT.

At Newport Police-court on Friday John M'Lean, aged 39, a builder and contractor, now living at Hopewell-hill, Kingswood-hill, Bristol, was charged in custody with assaulting his father-in-law, Mr. John Hyndman, landlord of the Old Ship Inn, and his brother-in-law, Mr. William Downing Hyndman, on Thursday evening.— Mr. W. Lyndon Moore appeared for the prosecution, and explained that the prisoner, who was some years ago married to Mr. Hyndman's daughter, very much against his wish, was now treating his wife very badly, and she had returned to her father's house. M'Lean had come there several times to her, and created disturbances. On Thursday night he went to the house, and, having forced his way into the private house behind the bar, went into the room where Mr. Hyndham, who was an invalid 77 years of age, was sitting. Mr. Hyndman ordered him out, but he refused to go, and on Mr. Hyndman trying to put him out, defendant kicked him and seized his son, who went to his father's assistance, by the throat.—Defendant said he considered he had a right there to see his wife and child, especially as he was managing a business for his wife and wanted her to sign a document.—Mr. Hyndman said he only wanted protection.—The Bench decided to impose a fine of 21s. and to bind defendant over to keep the peace, or in default a month's imprisonment.

South Wales Daily News, 11 March 1893

contractor, had married four years earlier. He and his wife Mary had a baby daughter, Lucy.

However, on 11 March 1893, about two years after their brief residence in Spring Cottage, the *South Wales Daily News* reported that the marriage had been *"very much against his will"*. McLean, as the newspaper spelt his name, was now treating his wife very badly. She had *"returned to her father's house"*, not for the first time, taking their child with her.

The house in question was a pub in Newport, the Old Ship, where McLean had caused trouble previously when visiting Mary. This time, he was charged with assaulting his elderly father-in-law (the pub landlord), John Hyndman, and his brother-in-law, William Hyndman.

He kicked the 77-year-old publican as he sat in a private room behind the bar and grabbed the younger man by the throat when he tried to intervene. Newport's magistrates fined McLean 21 shillings and bound him over to keep the peace, or face prison.

It comes as some surprise, therefore, to find the couple still together two decades later. The 1911 Wales Census listed the McLeans as living in Cockett, near Swansea – having produced five more children, all girls, to total six daughters in all.

CHARLES FRANKLIN – GLASSWORKS FIRE

During most of the 1890s, Spring Cottage was given a street number for the first time – number 50. In March 1892 an advertisement appeared in the *Western Daily Press*, offering the whole site for rent: *"To Let; Spring Cottage, 50 Fairfield road, Montpelier; eight rooms, south aspect, pleasant, healthy; Lawn, greenhouse, good garden and stable. Rent £200 - apply on premises."*

One person who did apply was Charles Franklin. His is another dramatic story involving a tenant of Spring Cottage. Franklin, a 32-year-old glass mirror manufacturer, lived there from 1893 to 1894.[51] He was married to a woman named Fanny (an abbreviation of Frances), and they had a 10-year-old daughter, Rosa Florence, when the family moved in.

Charles Franklin ran a large factory manufacturing glass products, the Albion Works in Rupert Street. It had 40 employees, mainly producing mirrors for shops and the home. Two years earlier, in 1891, it had been gutted by a devastating fire that ripped through the premises, including a block that was six storeys high. A report in the *Bristol Mercury* on 17 March gave a vivid account of flames, fanned by a strong wind, shooting 30 feet above the burning roof in one of the city's most destructive blazes for years.

The fire started in a boiler room which powered the whole works. It drew spectators from all over the city, with many watching from the hillsides of Clifton, Redland and Cotham. Workers inside had fled for their lives as smoke filled the stairwells. According to the *Mercury* report, one of the buildings was especially inflammable because it had once been a sugar factory, and the floors

NOTHING COULD SAVE THE BUILDING.

The flames, fed by the inflammable contents of the piece, became brighter and brighter, and poured out of every doorway and window with an intensity of heat which drove back the firemen and spectators from time to time, and was felt by persons working in the upper storeys of buildings some considerable distance away. Crash after crash was heard as floor after floor gave way in both blocks, and the heavy machinery, including the large stones used in the bevelling departments, fell carrying everything to the ground. Before eight o'clock the roof of the lower block had collapsed, and a little later the fire had gone up through the higher premises. As the second roof gave way several of the coping stones fell into Rupert street, and the firemen had to exercise great care to secure their personal safety. By this time the newly constituted brigade at Horfield had arrived, under Mr Hucker, and they rendered considerable assistance to the police brigades, who continued working in great danger from threatening roofs and walls. The scene as the upper roof fell in was one of weird grandeur, the flames shooting up above the six-storeyed building to a height of 30 feet, and pouring out of all the windows on every side, whilst a tremendous shower of sparks deluged the surrounding neighbourhood,

Bristol Mercury, 17 March 1891

were saturated with sugar and treacle. Franklin himself was away in Cardiff, buying new plant and machinery.

The report added that by the time firemen had extinguished the blaze, only the bare walls were left standing. There had been an unusually large quantity of stock on the premises. Some 250 finished overmantels, as well many other unfinished ones, and several hundred *"toilet glasses"*, were all destroyed. Damage was put at between £4,000 and £5,000, but Franklin was only partially insured. His entire 40-strong workforce lost their jobs.

The city is still famous now for its Bristol Blue Glass, but for centuries this was just one part of a huge local glass-making industry. In a book about selected well-known products manufactured locally, David Bolton gives an indication of that industry's importance:

"The city's skyline was once dotted with all-brick conical glass-making furnaces. In the eighteenth century more than 60 glasshouses made over half the bottles and window glass in Britain." [52]

However, as Bolton points out, during the latter part of the nineteenth century, glassmaking in Bristol went into decline. Charles Franklin's Albion Works served a niche market for high-quality skilled craftsmanship, although until the fire he had recently been expanding production. The works specialised in making mirrors, overmantels and cabinets with finely bevelled glass.

The fire could have destroyed his business permanently, but Franklin found a way to recover. During his time living at Spring Cottage, he began setting up a new and smaller enterprise, manufacturing some new mirrors, but also refurbishing old ones.

Eventually, Franklin was ready to open a new workshop in the city centre, at Wesley Place in the Horsefair. It was advertised by the *Bristol Magpie* on 8 July 1897:

Send your OLD MIRRORS to be RE-SILVERED.

— — —

CHARLES FRANKLIN,
The Original
Looking Glass Manufacturer,
From Rupert Street, Removed to
ALBION WORKS,
WESLEY PLACE, HORSEFAIR,
BRISTOL.
Specialities.—Shop Mirrors, Glass Shelves, Re-silvering. Re-gilding, Bevelling & Silvering
If you want any of the above, a postcard will ensure attention.

Wright's Directory for 1894 recorded that by then Charles Franklin and his family had moved from Spring Cottage to Beaufort House in Berkeley Road, about a mile away in Bishopston. It was to remain their home for the next 15 years, with Franklin continuing his business in the Horsefair. He died in 1913, at the age of 52.

Beaufort House (now Berkeley House) in Berkeley Road, Bishopston. Charles Franklin and his family lived here for 15 years after Spring Cottage. (Photo: Paul Bullivant)

LEE AND FOOT - A TALE OF TWO BUTCHERS

In his will the owner of Spring Cottage and adjoining house since 1872, local butcher Henry Lee, decided his wife Emma would not inherit the property. Instead, on his death in 1898, he left it to another butcher, Henry Foot, who was also his nephew.[53] Foot's address in the Censuses of both 1881 and 1891 was given as 21 Milk Street in St Pauls, a district bordering Montpelier.

The Lee family had been butchers a few doors along from Foot, at 14 Milk Street, since at least 1828. According to Mathews' Directory, it was Henry's father, William Lee , who started trading from there. William was still at 14 Milk Street in 1849. However, in 1871 the butcher at that address was listed as Henry Lee. By then Henry must have taken over the Lee family business.

The two Henrys, Lee and Foot, had a close personal and business relationship, based literally on nepotism. Foot was over 30 years younger than his uncle. He was described in some of our house deeds as a *"farmer"*, then later as a *"butcher and cattle dealer"*.

Instead of inheriting the Spring Cottage premises on her husband's death

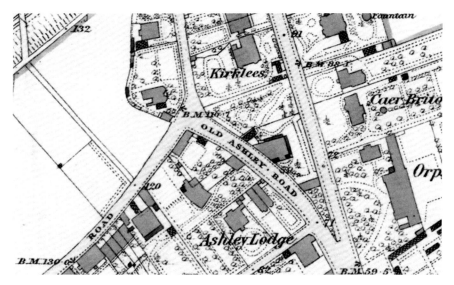

1844-1888 OS 25" 1st Edition. This map, surveyed by the Ordnance Survey in 1881 using the latest mapping techniques, shows more detail of gardens and paths, but few additional buildings since the 1855 Ashmead map.

in 1898, Emma Lee was left an annuity of £150 for her upkeep elsewhere. She died 20 years later, in 1918.

The butchers were so close that Henry Foot named all three of his sons after his uncle, calling them "Henry Walter Lee Foot", "Thomas Lee Foot" and "Edwin Lee Foot". Henry Foot and his wife Elizabeth also had a daughter, Clara Rachel, who was to be gifted Spring Cottage in 1909. As far as we know, none of these owners ever lived here.

RESEARCHING THE PEOPLE WHO LIVED IN YOUR HOUSE - LATE NINETEENTH CENTURY

This was the time of massive Victorian housing development in British cities. Bristol grew especially rapidly from 1860 onwards. Large suburbs of terraced housing and semi-detached homes for the better off were built, as the city boundaries expanded out into the countryside. The terraces, of variable quality for workers, were built close to factories and workplaces. These were also usually nearer the city centre, whereas larger detached houses and semis were built further out in the leafier suburbs. Victorian housing was also built in districts like Montpelier and Clifton, between the older and larger Georgian houses.

Spring Cottage/60 Fairfield Road became surrounded by terraced housing at the very end of the century. (See Chapter 5.) Private companies, usually small building firms, bought up the land to erect these houses. They then sold them on to relatively rich people, who often let them to poorer tenants. It was common for families to be much larger than the average now. With children, additional family members such as cousins and grandparents, plus lodgers and young servants, many households became very overcrowded by modern standards. This, of course, may provide a lot more stories for the house historian to discover.

The Census really comes into its own for researching this period. Ancestry and Find My Past websites, as mentioned already, are well worth exploring for census and many other types of records. The whole administrative process of conducting an organised and accurate census was much improved by this time, and the records become more productive to search online. You can search by names, dates and street or house name. However, bear in mind these may well have changed over time. For example, our house changed its name to Spring Villa for a while during this era. Fairfield Road wasn't yet fully established as an address either, making a search more difficult. Census enumerators, who travelled around the city collecting the information on the ground, weren't always completely accurate. Their spelling of names for a person, house or street could be misleading or plain wrong. It's therefore useful, as well as interesting, to study not just transcriptions, but also the images of the original records. Sometimes you might recognise a mangled handwritten name, which was then transcribed incorrectly, but fits with other evidence you've collected. Then, suddenly, the jigsaw comes together. Another check you can make is to compare the list of records made by the enumerators with the **street map**. You can work out which direction they were walking from the order of the property listings, and so ensure you have the right house.

Newspapers are a very useful resource for this period, allowing you to build up a much richer picture of the lives of your house occupants. Their misfortunes, such as the terrible fire in the glass factory which nearly ruined Charles Franklin, are often well (and sometimes luridly) documented in the local papers. If they got into trouble with the law, like John McLean, who assaulted his father-in-law in Newport, there it is in shaming detail. As described at the end of the previous chapter, further information about people's criminal activity can be found in several **online resources** and in your **local Archives**. However, more mundane matters are also commonly featured in the papers. People used them to communicate everything from the sale of garden tools to announcements of marriage. The **British Newspaper Archive** https://www.britishnewspaperarchive.co.uk/ and your local reference library or Archives will again give you extensive access.

By this time, **Trade and Street Directories** were well developed and commonly used. They're available to search, either by name of person or by address. Alphabetical lists of people offering a particular type of service or goods are also found in trade directories. In Bristol the central **Reference Library** and **Bristol Archives** have a very good collection of these directories, which you can read on the premises. The Bristol library has many other resources which the house historian may also find invaluable. They include: old maps; collections of local photographs and illustrations; newspapers from 1704 onwards on microfilm; electoral registers and oral histories. Generally, reference libraries complement the facilities in your local Archives and are well worth exploring.

CHAPTER 5

FIRST HALF OF TWENTIETH CENTURY

SHRINKING GARDEN

Up to now, everyone living on the Spring Cottage premises had benefited from having a large garden sloping down Old Ashley Hill from the top. Only a relatively small part of the land bought by Jacob Crook had been built on. So, the garden stretched as far as the next house, Green Bank Cottage (since demolished), and from our home there must have been fine views down the hill to the countryside beyond.

Nowadays, our front door lies on Fairfield Road. However, in the 1800s, we believe, the front door was what has since become the back one on the garden side. When we moved to Montpelier in 1986, there was also still a door into the old cottage end of our house from the garden. Indeed, the back of the whole house used to be its front – and still looks like it.

Suddenly, in 1898, the garden of Spring Cottage was reduced by at least half by a new housing development on Old Ashley Hill. The new owner, Henry Foot, sold much of his remaining land that had not been built on to a neighbouring builder and developer, William Scott. The latter constructed three terraced houses there, forming part of a longer terrace down the hill.[54]

Fairfield Road, too, was getting more built up, and no longer lived up to its name. There had been a rush of new house building since the 1880s. Gone were the days when Spring Cottage stood in splendid isolation. (See the map on page 89.)

There was plenty to attract families to live in Fairfield Road. Montpelier now had its own station, completed in 1874, on the new railway line from Bristol's main station, Temple Meads, to Clifton Down. Even on this limited

Garden and rear view of 60 Fairfield Road in December 2019. There was a door to the original cottage, now blocked up, under the dogleg formed by the drainpipe on the right. (Photo: Paul Bullivant)

Our back door from the garden used to be the front door.

The first houses in the terrace down Old Ashley Hill were built in 1898, just below 60 Fairfield Road.

route there were 46 trains running every day, 23 each way.[55]

The line had been extended to Avonmouth in 1885, after the opening of a tunnel at Clifton Down. These frequent trains, stopping at Montpelier, provided an important new transport link for a large number of passengers, including those travelling to and from work. It meant, too, that people could escape more easily from the city to semi-rural places outside Bristol for a day out.

Public education in Montpelier was also improving. Colston Girls' Day School had opened in 1891, and soon filled all 300 places. It was funded by the

1894-1903 OS 25" 2nd Edition. This Ordnance Survey map, surveyed in 1902, shows the many new houses in Fairfield Road, Old Ashley Hill and nearby streets. The new Fairfield School is also marked.

Fairfield School opened in 1898 and was soon for secondary age pupils only. They included local boy and future Hollywood film star Cary Grant, then known by his real name Archie Leach. (Photo: Julian Plested)

Edward Colston Trust and administered by the Society of Merchant Venturers. Then, at the end of the century, the residents of Fairfield Road gained a brand new school almost on their doorstep. The co-educational Fairfield Higher Grade School opened in 1898, with over 1,000 pupils.[56]

Ashley Hill in the early 1920s, looking towards Old Ashley Hill (branching left further up). The row of shops on the left include a bakery and a grocer's, either side of the junction with Lower Cheltenham Place. There's a newsagent's on the right. All these shops have since gone. (Photo: Bristol Archives 43207/9/21/84)

Eventually, after more than a century as a secondary school, its buildings would become outdated by modern standards and the cramped site inadequate for so many children. Fairfield School then closed and a major high-quality renovation was carried out, while keeping its Victorian architectural design. It re-opened as Fairlawn Primary School in 2015.

Other developments, from around the turn of the twentieth century, included more shops opening to serve the new larger community, both on Fairfield Road and on Ashley Hill.

ADA TOVEY – CHILD SERVANT

While Henry Foot was still the owner, the 1901 Census gave details of a new family, the Moffatts, as tenants at *"60 Fairfield Road"*. It was one of the earliest examples of that address being officially used for our house. This may also have signalled the beginning of its unification into one family home, rather than two.

William Moffatt (37), originally from Nottinghamshire, was the superintendent of a wire netting works. The other family members were: his wife Sarah (40), from Westmoreland, and their three children, all boys and all born in Bristol. They were called William, aged 12, Charles (7) and baby Frederick. The family had a 13-year-old live-in servant, Ada Tovey.

In 1903, while still living at 60 Fairfield Road, William and Sarah Moffatt had a fourth child (their only girl), whom they named Dorothy.

It was not unusual at the time for an ordinary family to have at least one servant, and to employ a girl as young as 13 in that role. The Moffatts' servant at 60 Fairfield Road, Ada Tovey, had lost her father, Charles Tovey, when she was about seven and a baby brother, George, when she was three. The father, originally from Cheltenham, had worked as a joiner but died young.

According to the 1901 Census, Ada's widowed mother, Mary, a nurse and midwife then aged 40, was living at 13 Haversham Street in the nearby district of Barton Hill. She shared her home with her 16-year-old son Frank, who worked as an *"errand boy [at the] Port"* and later became a soldier.

The same Census reveals that Ada's older sister Lilian, who was 18, also had employment as a live-in servant – to the Roberts family, just a few doors away from Ada, at 52 Fairfield Road. They were a married couple with two children.

Ada's employers, William and Sarah Moffatt, needed a servant to look after their four children and keep house at number 60. Having her older sister doing a similar job so close by must have provided great comfort to the 13 year old and companionship for both.

In 1905 the Moffatt family moved a very short distance away, to 17 Hurlingham Road. It was just the other side of the railway line and reached by a brand new footbridge. We don't know whether Ada continued working for that family in their new home. By 1911, however, the Moffatts no longer had any servant as part of their household.

Meanwhile, Lilian was still in that role, now with the Chapman family and again in a neighbouring house to the Moffatts, 5 Hurlingham Road. Her sister's presence there suggests that Ada did, indeed, continue with the Moffatts, at least at first, after they left 60 Fairfield Road.

ADA IN CANADA

Later in that same year, life for both Tovey sisters and their mother changed completely. Like many other working class Bristol people, even those with jobs, they were desperately poor. In October 1911 Ada Tovey, now a young woman of 23, emigrated to Canada with her mother Mary and sister Lilian to start a new life across the Atlantic. Ship passenger lists for sailings from the Port of Bristol show they boarded a vessel, the *Royal Edward*, bound for Quebec.[57] Their passage had been paid for, under a charity scheme for emigrants, by the Salvation Army.

All three Toveys' names also appear on a Canadian list of passengers, newly arrived in Montreal on 25 October. "S. ARMY" is stamped next to each of their names on the document. Their end destination was given as Vancouver, on the opposite west coast of this huge country. Ada and Lilian both stated that finding employment there, again as domestic servants, was their aim. Their mother Mary hoped to use her previous experience to work as a nurse.

However, Ada's escape route may have proved to be a blind alley. An entry in the British Columbia Death Index refers to the death of a young woman called Ida Tovey, in Vancouver on 27 July 1912, aged 24. If "Ida" is a misspelling, it means that Ada reached her end destination, but survived for less than a year after the family's arrival in Canada. We've found no identifiable record of what happened to her mother and sister.[58]

The Toveys were by no means unusual in becoming British emigrants to Canada. In the early twentieth century, it was the most popular destination in an unprecedented wave of emigration from these shores, driven by poverty. Over three million people left Britain between 1903 and 1913, in the hope of a better life overseas. Of these, almost half went to Canada.[59]

Of course, many of the British emigrants had children with them. However, some young ones had to make the perilous journey across the Atlantic alone. *Bristol's Pauper Children*, a book by Shirley Hodgson, tells the story of how more than 1,500 destitute children from Bristol were transported to Canada in the late 1800s and early 1900s.

The children were sent from Bristol workhouses and other institutions for the poor, sometimes by their own parents, to work as extra farm labourers or as

A group of English immigrants in Quebec in 1908 (Photo: Library and Archives Canada)

servants for Canadian families. It's estimated that around 60,000 Canadians of the present day are descended from these young Bristol paupers.[60]

Many emigrant families, however, like the Toveys, received help from the Salvation Army in their passage to Canada. A study by York University in Toronto has put the total of British emigrants, funded by the charity to reach Canada up to 1930, at around 200,000. A large proportion of them, like Ada's mother, were widows accompanied by their offspring. However, they were resented by some Canadians, who thought Britain was dumping its poorest people in Canada.[61]

MALTHOUSE MYSTERY

According to the 1901 Census, there was a *"malthouse"* on our premises, which it described as being *"in occupation"* – so presumably in active use. However, none of the Moffatt family, who lived at 60 Fairfield Road at the time, worked in the brewing trade. The next Census, in 1911, made no mention of the malthouse, nor can we find it in any other document from any period.

Could the Census authors have been alluding instead to a much larger

The former malthouse off Fairlawn Road, now converted into apartments

commercial malthouse and oast house, built only a couple of hundred yards away off Fairlawn Road? It was opened in 1876 by Cyril Pillers, a maltster and hop merchant living with his family in Rockley Villa, which was one of the nearest houses to Spring Cottage along Fairfield Road.[62]

On the other hand, several local maps, from the mid nineteenth century until well into the twentieth, did show for the first time an outbuilding in the part of our garden adjoining Old Ashley Hill. It featured on the 1855 and 1874 Ashmead maps of Bristol, and also on the first three Ordnance Survey editions covering 1881 to 1912.

However, this outbuilding was more likely to have been a glasshouse, since it was symbolised on the maps with cross hatching. There were also several references to a glasshouse, or greenhouse, on the premises in local newspaper advertisements of the time:

Advertisement in the Western Daily Press, 11 September 1880

The outbuilding in our garden may have been used as a malthouse in the early 1900s. (Photo: Paul Bullivant)

There's one further possibility. Another outbuilding still stands at the opposite end of our garden. It was erected in about 1900, just before the Census of 1901. (We've since converted it into a modern living space.) This outbuilding could have been used as a small malthouse by tenants to brew their own beer, and maybe was built partly for that purpose. It's only a theory, but would explain the Census reference to a malthouse, *"in occupation"*, on our site.

BEERS ALL ROUND

Despite the conflicting evidence over a malthouse, there's definitely a strong beery thread running through this history, but it's hard to pin down. 60 Fairfield Road, as it eventually became known, was first built by a maltster (Shurmer Bath), then a brewer (Jacob Crook).

Past owners of the land before it was built on, since the seventeenth century, included a brewer called Andrew Hooke and a distiller by the name of George Bridges (the latter also yet another Quaker).[63] The Viner family, tenants for many years in the mid 1800s, were an assortment of hop merchants, brewers, maltsters and travelling beer salesmen.

Yet this brewing dominance would have seemed quite normal to any Bristolian, or indeed anyone in England, until well into the twentieth century. Before 1800 the city had many small local breweries supplying 600 or so pubs. For hundreds of years, beer was cheap and most people drank huge quantities. As David Bolton puts it in his book, *Made in Bristol:*

"There was a very good reason for this. It was probably better for them than the local drinking water, which was often heavily contaminated...As a result most English families, including children, drank beer for breakfast, lunch and dinner."

For much of the nineteenth and twentieth centuries, George's Brewery, in the city centre, bought up its main competitors one by one. Bordering Montpelier stood the Stokes Croft Brewery, on the corner of City Road and Stokes Croft, but it was eventually also taken over by George's in the early 1900s.[64]

This was a late nineteenth century advertisement for ales from the Stokes Croft Brewery. (Image: courtesy of Brewery History Society.)

In the new millennium, micro breweries, or craft breweries, have made a comeback in Bristol. They're springing up locally in all sorts of tiny premises, especially in Stokes Croft, St Werburghs and Ashley Down.

CLARA'S HOUSE

In 1909 Henry Foot transferred the ownership of Spring Cottage (this time again meaning the whole property) to his daughter. Clara Foot was only 26, and the youngest owner in its history up to then. She was also married, with her surname changed to Leigh. A legal indenture between father and daughter also gave Clara six pounds a year in ground rent, for each of the three new terraced houses built on the garden land sold off by Henry. She was entitled to this, by some legal quirk, even though the land was freehold.[65]

By then, Henry Foot had moved from Milk Street in St Pauls to 149 Cheltenham Road, on the edge of Montpelier, while Clara lived nearby at 40 Cranbrook Road in Redland. Her husband, William Leigh, was a travelling salesman. The couple had a son, also William, born in the following year, 1910.

The 1911 Census described Clara's father, at the age of 56, as having *"private means"*. We can assume Foot had made enough money to retire early, most likely from selling the garden land at 60 Fairfield Road. His eldest son, Henry Walter Lee Foot, had gone into the butcher's trade as well, so Henry senior could hand over the family business to him.

By now, Henry Foot senior's wife Elizabeth had died, and he was married to his second wife, Mary. But why did he gift Spring Cottage to Clara rather than his eldest son, who was three years older than her?

Perhaps Foot reckoned he had already done enough for Henry and wanted Clara provided for, too. Our house deeds include a later legal document of 1925, in which Henry Foot is said to have acted *"in consideration of his natural love and affection for his daughter"*.

EVELYN ANNIE WARREN – CAREER WOMAN

In 1905, when the Moffatts moved across the railway track to Hurlingham Road, they were replaced by another family, the Warrens, as tenants at 60 Fairfield Road. The new household, as later recorded in the 1911 Census, was headed by Alfred Warren, a middle-aged South African born in Port Elizabeth.

Alfred worked as cashier to a wholesale clothing firm called Dickie, Parsons and Co in Nelson Street. His wife Annie came originally from Nottingham.

Bristol University's iconic landmark, the Wills Memorial Building, was opened in 1925, soon after Evelyn Annie Warren's time as a mature student. (Photo: Paul Bullivant)

They had their 21-year-old daughter, Evelyn Annie, living with them. She was single, with a job as a junior assistant librarian for the Bristol City Corporation.

Soon after the First World War, Evelyn Annie Warren began a course at Bristol University. On 25 June 1919, the *Western Daily Press* included her name in a list of women who had passed a *"first examination for the testamur in social study"* at the University. Evelyn Annie was one of only three women listed. She was now a mature student of 29, her career plans no doubt interrupted by the war.

A request to the University's Special Collections team of archivists has yielded further information. The Testamur [certificate] in Social Study was introduced at Bristol in 1912 as a vocational course for people intending to become social, welfare or charity workers, or for those seeking a personnel job in government or industry. It involved two years of study, and Evelyn Annie must have completed the first part.

Bristol University keeps an archive of all past students, exam results and graduates. Unfortunately, there is a gap in the lists from 1918 to 1922, and they can find no record of Evelyn Annie Warren. We therefore don't know whether she ever completed her course and gained the qualification.

It was still unusual in that era for any woman from an ordinary background to go to university at all. However, there are grounds for believing that maybe Evelyn Annie did achieve her certificate, and that her studies eventually led to employment in a relevant field.

The Warren family was still at 60 Fairfield Road in December 1921, when the *Western Daily Press* reported her mother's *"sudden"* death at home. Evelyn

Annie and her widowed father later both moved away to Bolton in Lancashire where, according to the 1939 Register, they were living together around the start of the Second World War.

Alfred Warren had retired, while Evelyn Annie, now 49, was working as an *"Industrial Welfare Superintendent"* in a cotton mill. Few women back then would have been considered for a management role in the textile industry. A university qualification was, perhaps, one way for her to land the job.

Alfred Warren was 80 when he died the following year, 1940. Evelyn Annie never married and died in 1967, at the age of 77.

RICHARD WARE – FIRST OWNER OCCUPIER

In 1925 Clara Leigh, now living at 36 Burghley Road in St Andrews, sold her property in Montpelier. This time it was described in the conveyance document as"*58 and 60 Fairfield Road*", with no mention of Spring Cottage. The buyer was Richard Ware. It had already been his home as a tenant for about three years. Richard now became the first owner since its early days to live there himself.

Richard Ware was a young man in his twenties, from the Knowle area of Bristol, recently discharged as a clerk in the Navy after the First World War. He had moved to Fairfield Road in 1922 with his new wife Muriel (maiden name Ivey), who was from Kildare in Ireland. The couple had a son, John, in October the same year, while living in our house. By then, Richard was working as a commercial manager in the fruit trade.

Our deeds relate that the very next day after completing his house purchase, on 21 October 1925, Richard Ware signed a mortgage agreement with Tripp and Arthur Adams, potato merchants in Lawrence Hill. They were an uncle and nephew from a long-established family firm, who also ran fruit and veg stalls in Bristol's central St Nicholas Market and a greengrocer's shop.[66]

Richard, who sold fruit himself for a living, borrowed £375 from the Adams pair, presumably so that he could afford the house purchase. In return, Tripp and Arthur were given use of the premises, on condition that Richard maintained them in a good state.

It's not clear why, but the most likely reason was so the Adams family could

Fruit and veg merchants Tripp and Arthur Adams may have stored potatoes in this outbuilding on Fairfield Road in the mid 1920s.

store potatoes and/or fruit in the outbuilding off Fairfield Road, alongside our house. They already had a potato store at 33 and 35 Lawrence Hill, but may have needed extra space. The outbuilding was probably new at the time. It had been built as an extension to the slightly older one in our garden mentioned before, which may have served as a malthouse.

The arrangement with Tripp and Arthur Adams proved short-lived. In 1927 Richard Ware sold his property to Anton Sunderland, a building contractor from nearby Horfield. In the conveyance document it was described as a *"dwelling house, garage and premises known as Spring Cottage and numbered 58 and 60 Fairfield Road"*. The garage must have been that same outbuilding.

Almost a decade later, after moving to another part of Bristol, the Wares had a second child, Jennifer, in 1936. However, soon afterwards, Richard and Muriel separated. In 1941 she took him to court, on the grounds of desertion. In 1946 Richard married again, and he lived on into old age.

ERNEST FIDDES - KILLED IN ACTION

In 1928 the house changed ownership again. Our deeds tell us it was bought by 41-year-old Ernest Herbert Alfred Fiddes. He ran a general stores in Wellesley

HMS Tempest in 1941 (Photo: from Imperial War Museum collections, copyright IWM)

Street, Lawrence Hill, and also traded as a glass cutter. Ernest Herbert was known as Bert to family and friends. For the next 30 years, various members of the Fiddes family lived in what, at first, was still called 58 and 60 Fairfield Road. They were struck by tragedy during the Second World War.

In the 1939 Register, Ernest "Bert" Fiddes and his wife Minnie, or "Min", were listed as still being at the same premises, but now there was just one house number instead of two – number 60. They had a grown-up son, aged about 24 and also named Ernest Herbert Alfred (but known as Ern). Their daughter Betty, aged about 12, was presumably living with them. However, the Register had one hidden entry for 60 Fairfield Road, marked *"this entry is officially closed"*, which may refer to her.

When Ern was called up for war service, he joined the Royal Navy. In February 1942, Stoker Petty Officer Ernest Fiddes was a member of the crew on board a submarine, *HMS Tempest*, in the Mediterranean.

HMS TEMPEST

On 23 February, during a patrol from its base in Malta, *HMS Tempest* reached the Gulf of Taranto off south eastern Italy. Then it was spotted on the surface by an Italian torpedo boat, or destroyer, *Circe*. The submarine crash dived, and

Stoker Petty Officer Ernest Fiddes, who died in the sinking of HMS Tempest on 23 February 1942.
(Photo: courtesy of John Apperley)

Circe began depth charging the area.

Tempest's battery tanks were ruptured, filling the vessel with chlorine gas and forcing her to re-surface. She was then hit by gunfire from *Circe*, until the surviving crew had to abandon her. Of the 62 men on board, 24 were picked up by the torpedo boat after several hours in the water. One survivor died later from his wounds. *HMS Tempest* sank as the Italians tried to take her in tow.

A total of 39 crew members lost their lives, including Stoker Petty Officer Fiddes, either from drowning or being hit by gunfire. Ern, apparently also known as "Eddie" by some of his crewmates in the Navy, was 27 years old. He was later mentioned in dispatches for gallant action in the face of the enemy – one of two men (both stokers) to be honoured for their conduct during the attack.[67]

The term 'stoker' was a leftover from the days of steam ships, when men literally shovelled coal into furnaces to fuel them. By the Second World War, submarines had become diesel electric powered, with diesel engines to propel them on the surface and batteries for when submerged. The stoker's role had changed to more that of a marine engineer or technician, responsible for the smooth running of its propulsion systems.

HMS Tempest was a brand new 'T' class submarine, completed only a few months earlier at the Cammell Laird shipyard in Birkenhead. She was thought to be stronger than other submarines and better at withstanding attack. *Tempest* had orders to sail for the Mediterranean on New Year's Day 1942, with her own crew on board. They had been fully trained together as a team since she was built.

Dave Hanson is a descendant of one *Tempest* crew member who survived the sinking, Petty Officer Eric Campbell. Dave has set up a website dedicated to the memory of his great uncle and his naval career. It also features the recollections of other survivors from the *Tempest*. [68]

One of these men recalled how, just hours before departure from Britain, most of the 62-strong crew who had been involved in trials and testing of the new submarine were taken off *Tempest* for *"other important duties"*. A new crew *"very hastily arrived"*, some of whom even had to jump aboard as *Tempest* set sail.

Percie Cooke was one of those crew members taken off the submarine. He had been reluctant to leave and had pleaded to stay on board. Cooke was a friend of Ernest (or "Eddie") Fiddes. From Cooke's very moving testimony, it's clear that Ern was on the fateful voyage purely by chance:

"It was Eddie Fiddes who came along to replace me, an old friend I knew where we served together on our first submarine, HMS Cachalot, at the beginning of the war. It must have been fate that day because Eddie was not among the survivors after the terrible depth-charging. It could so easily have been me."

FINAL HOURS OF HMS TEMPEST

We've found no record of what Stoker Petty Officer Fiddes did as an individual to warrant being posthumously mentioned in dispatches.

However, another survivor from *HMS Tempest*, Coxswain Charles Anscomb, later wrote a graphic account of the sinking in his book *Submariner*.

In one passage from the memoir, Anscomb described how all 15 stokers on board - about a quarter of the entire crew - bravely tried to save their vessel as it was being hit by depth-charges from the Italian destroyer.

"The master gyroscope was smashed and we had to rely on our magnetic compass. One oil fuel bulkhead connection in the control room was damaged and its oil fuel poured into the boat. The chief stoker, George Spowart, and his men got to it quickly and soon stopped the flood. The electrical artificer, John Winrow, slaved to put the gyro right, but it was past all hope of repair and we had to give it up...We were at the mercy of that destroyer...

"I know that no-one, least of all the young submariners who had been civilians

A survivor from the crew of HMS Tempest is picked up from the sea by Italian rescuers after the submarine was sunk by an enemy destroyer in February 1942. (Photo: Histomania)

only a few months before, showed the slightest sign of panic or fear. They all behaved splendidly...

"About 10.30 am the battery security boards showed signs of lifting. A closer inspection showed that salt water had got into the battery department and several containers, with sulphuric acid in them, were broken. When salt water and sulphuric acid mix they give off chlorine gas. This is the ultimate horror of all submariners.

"The boat started to fill with it. One whole battery was flooded now. We had reached the end, with no instrument working except 'faithful Freddie' the magnetic compass. What use was a compass now? Tempest had nowhere to go any more except to the bottom. At last, to save us going with her, the captain decided to abandon ship."[69]

The death of Ern Fiddes, at the age of 27 and in such dreadful circumstances,

was a terrible loss not only for his parents, Bert and Min, but also for his much younger sister, Betty. She was now 15 and had been brought up in Fairfield Road throughout the 1930s. Betty was a baby, and her brother about 13, when the Fiddes family moved in. They had Bert's older brother, Sam, as a neighbour, at 26 Fairfield Road, with his wife Lillian and their two children, who were Ern and Betty's cousins. Sam Fiddes owned a wholesale grocery business in Pennywell Road, St Philips.

Until 1935 Bert and Min shared their house with tenants William Bridgeman, who was a train driver, and his wife Edith. The latter gave birth to a son, Philip, during this period, in 1933. From then until 1938 or 1939, the Bridgemans were replaced as tenants by another couple, Henry (or Harry) and Ivy Barton. Harry worked as an upholsterer. The couple had a son, Brian, born in 1938. But he died while still a baby, soon after the Bartons left 60 Fairfield Road.[70]

After the war, Betty Fiddes carried on living with her parents in Montpelier for the next decade. When she married Maurice Whitcombe in 1952, he moved in, too. This arrangement continued until Betty's father, Bert, died in January 1957, aged 70.

His widow Min inherited the house from him, and then sold it the following year to Betty, whose surname was now Whitcombe. She and husband Maurice carried on living at 60 Fairfield Road, with her mother, until at least 1962.

Bert Fiddes in the early 1900s.

Bert was injured by gunfire as an Army serviceman in WW1.

Ern Fiddes (seated) with cousin Harold in the 1930s. Ern was to lose his life as a submariner in WW2.

A Fiddes Christmas party in Fairfield Road in the 1950s. The couple standing left are Min and Bert.

Bert's older brother, Sam (left), lived at 26 Fairfield Road from the 1920s, with his wife Lillian (right) and their two children.
(All photos on this page are courtesy of Ern's great niece, Sue Harris).

RESEARCHING THE PEOPLE WHO LIVED IN YOUR HOUSE – TWENTIETH CENTURY

Clues about who lived in your house in the twentieth century are often easier to find than in earlier periods. Your deeds may reveal names and dates as before, but people's memories of the 1900s can lead you to discover a bit more, especially if the house was lived in for a long time by the same family, over a couple of generations.

However, for extra information you'll probably need to research the records. Genealogy has become hugely popular. There's now a bewildering array of resources available online, as well as in various archives and libraries all over the world. There are some **free websites,** which usually have rather limited access to records, but may be a good starting point. They obviously cover a much wider range of dates than just the 1900s.

Examples of these free websites are:

- http://freeukgenealogy.org.uk which has census, parish, births, marriages and deaths records.
- http://findagrave.com which is a constantly growing record of graves all over the world.
- http://originsnetwork.com which provides links to documents like wills and apprenticeship records.
- http://cwgc.org The Commonwealth War Graves Commission.

However, you'll probably need to subscribe to one of the more comprehensive **paid-for websites** if you want to pursue your research more thoroughly. Ancestry and Findmypast have been used for this book, but others include:

- http://myheritage.com
- http://familyrelatives.com
- http://genesreunited.co.uk
- http://scotlandspeople.gov.uk

It may be worth exploring these sites because they contain a vast amount of searchable information - including military records, electoral registers and even ships' passenger lists, all of which were used in this chapter.

Censuses of the early twentieth century provide a bonus for researchers. The 1901 Census is available free online at http://ukcensusonline.com and the 1911 one can be viewed free online at the National Archives at Kew. The latter Census included British Army overseas personnel for the first time. Because of the '100 Year Rule' on data protection, the 1921 Census won't be available until 2022. There was a special census at the start of the Second World War - the 1939 England and Wales Register - which is available on Ancestry and Findmypast. However, there was no census in 1941 during the war.

Military records are clearly an important source because of the two World Wars, in which it's highly likely that some of your former residents took an active part. Much information can be found through the websites already mentioned. However, your local Archives will probably have good wartime collections. Bristol Archives has an extensive collection of local material relating to both World Wars, but it and counterparts elsewhere don't keep military service records. These are available through a variety of sources, on which the Imperial War Museum website provides a good overview: www.iwm.org.uk/research/tracing-your-family-history . A more specialist site for all this is http://forces-war-records.co.uk. Often, though, it's worth just trying a **Google** search. This is how some of the information about *HMS Tempest* and its crew was found for this chapter. People sometimes upload **memoirs** and personal archives to the internet. There are also specialist sites which focus on people's wartime memories. **Oral histories** may offer clues about changes to your local area during the twentieth century. Local libraries, museums or Archives will help you find interviews that have been recorded and transcribed.

Electoral Registers (also known as electoral rolls) are useful to identify at least some of the occupants of your house. Since 1843 they've listed annually those living at an address who are entitled to vote. They're found increasingly on websites like Ancestry and Findmypast, but not on the National Archives site. The British Library holds printed copies from 1947 onwards, as do the National Libraries of Wales and Scotland. In Bristol, both the central reference library and the Archives keep local electoral registers, but some years are missing.

The **Inland Revenue Valuation of 1910** was carried out to introduce a new tax on land values. These valuation books (held in local Archives and often known as the 1910 Domesday Books) give details of properties, their rateable values and owners and occupiers.

Photographs became far more common in the twentieth century. There are various ways of tracking these down, but sometimes a conversation with a longstanding neighbour or other locals can help you do so. The internet is obviously worth a try, and may reward you with surprisingly personal photos. The family tree sections of genealogy websites often contain images uploaded by people doing research on their own families. If you're lucky you may find one of interest to you. Your local Archives or reference library will have an extensive local photograph collection. Although it's less likely that you'll find photos of individuals, there may well be images of your street or the local neighbourhood from the early twentieth century. Bristol Archives holds several collections of old city photos. Many are now available on the Know Your Place mapping website http://www.kypwest.org.uk/. You can search for photos and other local information by finding your neighbourhood map, then exploring the 'Information Layers'.

CHAPTER 6
UP TO THE PRESENT DAY

A GEORGIAN HOUSE IN THE MODERN WORLD

Our house deeds tell us that in April 1961 Betty Whitcombe (*née* Fiddes) sold 60 Fairfield Road to a middle-aged married couple, Jack and Mabel Coleman. Even then, Betty, her husband Maurice and her mother, Min Fiddes, stayed on with the Colemans for another year. It had been Min's home for 34 years, since 1928.

When Jack Coleman, who was a window blind manufacturer, died in 1971 at the age of 54, his widow Mabel kept the house until 1979. During much of this period, after Jack's death, she had their grown-up sons, Guy and Geoffrey, and Guy's wife Diana, living with her.

In 1979 Mabel Coleman sold 60 Fairfield Road to two women, Penny Gane and Linda Hunter. They lived in the house as co-owners for the next five years. During that time Penny Gane, born and bred in Bristol, taught English and Drama at Nailsea Secondary School in North Somerset, where Linda was also a teacher.

PENNY TAKES CHARGE

The new joint owners obtained a council grant to renovate the house and convert it into flats, for Penny to live upstairs and Linda downstairs. They rewired the whole building themselves, re-fitted the kitchen and stripped doors to modernise the house, while keeping or restoring its original period features. There was the odd mishap along the way. After the rewiring, Penny says, at first every time they switched on a light the phone rang![71]

Penny Gane

This period fireplace was installed by Penny Gane. (Photo: Paul Bullivant)

The two women's work on the house in the early 1980s was largely responsible for how it still looks today. It was also an example of the gradual gentrification of the area. An influx of middle class home owners to that part of Bristol at the time saw them stripping away the changes made by traditional local families, who had lived there previously, and reverting to the original.

Moving on from 60 Fairfield Road in 1984, Penny Gane embarked on a stellar career in many fields. In the 1990s she helped to introduce recycling in Bristol and led the setting up of its centre for sustainable development, Create. Then, in 2012, she launched Bristol Women's Voice, after being commissioned to establish a network of women in Bristol to influence decision makers and tackle gender inequality.

In 2019 Penny had been chair of Bristol Women's Voice, and also the Bristol Mayoral Women's Commission, for about six years. During this time both organisations developed into an important factor in shaping policies for the city. She was invited to become a Fellow of the Royal Society for Arts in 2015, in recognition of her "outstanding work for women's equality". Earlier, she also helped to develop patient and public involvement in the health service.

The Create Centre was set up under Penny's leadership as head of sustainable development for Bristol City Council in the mid 1990s. It's in a

As chair of Bristol Women's Commission, Penny Gane addressed the Global Parliament of Mayors in October 2018. This was a gathering in Bristol of more than 80 civic leaders from six continents. They convened on pressing worldwide issues - migration, urban security and health. (Photo: courtesy of Penny Gane)

landmark converted building that was formerly one of the bonded warehouses in the city's Cumberland Basin. Owned and managed by the council, it provides workspace for several environmental organisations and a venue for seminars and conferences. Create also has its own purpose-built Ecohome, full of practical ideas for greener living, which is much visited by school groups.

Bristol Women's Voice, based in Brunswick Square, St Pauls, aims to support and empower women across the city. It promotes campaigns and events that advance female equality and rights, while also improving women's access to jobs and services. Women's Voice, funded by the council but independent of it, also helps women set up their own support networks.

In 2019 Penny also still chaired Bristol Women's Commission. This brings together leading figures from the council, industry, trade unions, both the city's universities, the police, the health service and the media, to ensure women are fully taken into account in strategic planning for the city. They draw up and implement action plans for key areas such as the economy, education, health and transport.

Penny and her husband, Nick Batchelor, now have three grown-up children. Nick is also a high-flyer, in his case in education. Like Penny he started as a teacher, and was appointed head of English at Gordano School in Portishead. He went on to lead the advisory service in Gloucestershire, before becoming director of education for Bristol and then Cardiff.

The Pavilion, designed by Marcel Breuer to showcase P.E. Gane furniture at the 1936 Royal Show in Bristol. (Photo: Archives of American Art, Smithsonian Institution)

THE BAUHAUS IN BRISTOL

Penny Gane's family has an illustrious past as well as present. She's the granddaughter of Crofton Gane, a Bristol furniture maker and retailer. His company, P.E. Gane, became a design trailblazer for Britain in the 1930s. It came about because of an unlikely friendship between Crofton, a passionate advocate of the Modernist movement, and Marcel Breuer, the celebrated architect and designer.[72]

Marcel Breuer was a founding member of the *Bauhaus* in Germany. The radical arts and crafts school at Weimar, which flourished between the two World Wars, was eventually forced to close down under Hitler's regime.

Breuer took refuge in London, where Crofton Gane met him and commissioned him to design a temporary pavilion for the Royal Agricultural Show in June 1936, held that year at Ashton Court in Bristol. The architect rated it as one of his finest works.

This original two-piece desk, designed by Marcel Breuer for P.E. Gane of Bristol in 1935, has been acquired for the Ken Stradling Collection.

Marcel and Crofton struck up a friendship which lasted for the rest of their lives. Breuer also designed furniture for the P.E. Gane company, and even remodelled the interior of Crofton's own family home, before settling in the United States.

Some of these designs by Breuer were showcased at a special exhibition in Bristol in late 2019, as part of the celebrations marking the *Bauhaus* centenary. It took place at the Ken Stradling Collection's gallery on Park Row.

However, the Second World War proved disastrous for Crofton Gane's furniture company. The P.E. Gane showroom at College Green, and its workshops, were destroyed in the bombing raids on Bristol of 1940. The business, whose roots in Bristol stretched back to the early nineteenth century, finally closed down in 1954.

Nevertheless, Crofton Gane has left an important long-term legacy. The *Bauhaus* furniture designs he championed in Bristol have since become a style classic, with an influence clearly visible if you go shopping today in home furnishing stores like Ikea. His great grandson (and Penny's son), Max Gane, has also carried on the family's design tradition by practising as an architect in the city.

Penny's parents were also highly creative people, her father as a

Crofton Gane (left) and Marcel Breuer in 1958
(Photo: Royal Institute of British Architects Collections)

photographer in Bristol and her mother a weaver. However, they struggled financially after the P.E. Gane closure and Penny experienced hardship, rather than privilege, as a child. She later won a free scholarship to the Red Maids School for girls in Bristol, which at the time was a charity school. Pupils there cleaned the classrooms before breakfast and slept in large cold dormitories.[73]

This quite tough upbringing makes her subsequent journey to prominence, via 60 Fairfield Road, all the more remarkable. Penny is clearly a natural leader, who has played a key role in shaping Bristol's future. But she combines enormous energy and dynamism with humour and warmth. Penny has made a real difference for women in Bristol and become one of the city's most influential voices on public policy. She sums herself up, more modestly, as a "feminist and activist".

After Penny Gane's and Linda Hunter's five years as 60 Fairfield Road residents, another woman became the next owner-occupier. Carolyn Britton, a lecturer in Social Policy at the University of the West of England, bought the house in 1984. Two years later it was ours, and has stayed that way ever since.

PAST AND PRESENT

By the end of 2019, my wife Sue and I had lived at 60 Fairfield Road for 33 years. This was longer than any previous residents, apart from Min Fiddes in the mid twentieth century.

The only major change on our watch has been to convert our outbuilding at the side of the house into a modern garage/shed and 'garden room'. It had previously stood detached from the main house, with an alleyway and outside door to the street. There's now an inside door, connecting our outbuilding to the house. The conversion, in 1994, also provided French windows overlooking the garden and an up-and-over door from Fairfield Road.

We had the steeply sloping cobbled floor of the outbuilding levelled off, recycled the cobbles into a patio outside the French windows and dug a small pond in the garden. Most recently, we've incorporated a new utility room into this area. When we first arrived, the house was rendered at the front and sides with a dingy grey pebbledash. The render has since been painted a warmer terracotta colour, using traditional limewash.

As we enter a new decade, the 2020s, I'm 66 and have retired after a career in journalism. I worked mainly as a news reporter or producer for BBC radio in Bristol and London, and for ITV Wales in Cardiff. As a farmer's son from Gloucestershire, I love the atmosphere in our house of a country cottage in the city. Like William Beaumont, one of its earliest tenants, I speak French, Spanish and Italian (although I've never taught them.)

My wife Sue shared our research for this project and wrote the tips on how to explore the past of your own house. She's originally from the North East and has retired from an academic career. Sue taught Geography in schools and colleges, before becoming a senior lecturer in Education at the Universities of Cardiff and the West of England.

The outbuilding in 1994 just before renovation, detached from the house.

Our son Tom has moved out of the family

Interior of the outbuilding in 1994.

The interior of the outbuilding after its conversion.

home into his own flat, also in Montpelier. Like a past resident in our house a century ago, Evelyn Annie Warren, he's now a librarian. Tom works at Bristol University, where Miss Warren was a student just after the First World War.

MISS NEWTH'S SCHOOL

Writing about the nineteenth century teachers, the Misses Phippen, reminded me of my own school days in Gloucestershire. They began in the late 1950s at Miss Newth's. This was a private day school for just 12 pupils, boys and girls from the age of four, run by Miss Newth from her own home. She lived in a small house in the town of Dursley and did all the teaching herself. Her ancient mother (or so she appeared to us), called Mrs Newth, sat in a corner of our classroom, benignly watching the lessons. It had been her school in the past. No one, not even our parents, used their first names. Everyone knew the school, very affectionately, just as "Miss Newth's".

My experience came at the tail end of a tradition stretching back to Mary and Charlotte Phippen, Mary Carpenter and their predecessors. They all ran private house schools. We were certainly not paupers at Miss Newth's, but middle class kids whose parents could afford the fees. Even Mary Carpenter, though, started as a teacher in the 1820s at her mother's house school on genteel Brandon Hill. Only later did she switch to the education of children from the poorest families.

RESEARCHING THE PEOPLE WHO LIVED IN YOUR HOUSE – RECENT RESIDENTS

If you've lived in your house for a long time, you may have lost all track of the people you bought it from. You probably never met them, so it's hard to find out much about the last occupants before you. Census records aren't available for most of the twentieth century either, so you may have to rely more on your **house deeds** for information. You will probably need to find these before you can start your research. Try your solicitor and/or the Land Registry.

The **Land Registry** https://www.gov.uk/government/organisations/land-registry is the legal repository for property ownership information in the UK. You may need to pay for a search.

The **Electoral Register,** which lists annually all those in a household eligible to vote, is available to view at http://192.com for 2002 onwards. Directory enquiries and births, marriages and deaths are also on this website.

Otherwise, you will need to use more **informal methods** to track down the names of former recent residents. There's an important caveat here - you obviously need to respect people's right to privacy and confidentiality. They may not want to respond to your requests for information, and they're perfectly entitled to do this. You must be sensitive and respectful, backing off as soon as you realise they aren't interested or willing to engage. Most people, however, are at least a little interested in their former home, and you may find they'll share some fascinating stories. For this house history, we knew from our deeds that Penny Gane was a past owner-occupier. A Google search confirmed she was a prominent figure in public life locally, which made it easier to contact her. Penny's response was enthusiastic and generous. She passed on some uniquely personal memories of 60 Fairfield Road.

Some ways of making contact with former residents that we used for this book are:

Conversations with friends and neighbours who may have known them. These can lead to clues like where they worked, or where they moved next.

Google searches can be very productive, sometimes revealing leads you may not have thought of. People's work is often the key. The internet can take you to an article written by them or about them, for example a blog. It gives you a better idea of their whereabouts, and possibly even an email address. Organisations are sometimes willing to pass on emails to the right person. This was how we made the initial contact with our past resident, Penny Gane.

Phone calls can be very helpful, because this is a more personal and direct way of making contact, and you can gauge the person's level of interest more easily.

Social media can open up other avenues. Linkedin, Facebook, Twitter, Instagram and other platforms enable quicker contact with people if they also use them. This is less likely with the older generation, but it's definitely worth trying.

Local print, broadcast and online media may also be a fruitful source of information about your former residents. Most have a search facility online.

Photographs of people are something you may come across in your investigations. It's important to seek their permission to use the photos if your findings are being published. Researching people who may still be around is different from historical research. It's vital to respect their right to privacy, confidentiality and anonymity. So tread carefully and happy researching!

CONCLUSION

The total number of people known, or thought, to have lived at Spring Cottage/60 Fairfield Road since before 1800 is about 100, but that's a conservative estimate. This history in no way provides a comprehensive record of all its residents. Our best guesstimate for the real total is well over 100, and perhaps far higher.

Changes in the social class of these residents over the years reflect a pattern for the whole of Fairfield Road and surrounding streets. The early tenants of Spring Cottage and adjoining house on our site, such as Miss Phippen and the extraordinary William Beaumont, tended to be quite well to do (and, in Beaumont's case, even aristocratic).

From the 1850s to the early 1900s, our residents were largely from the emerging lower middle class – commercial travellers, office clerks, middle managers, or small businessmen running their own company. After the First World War, owners of 60 Fairfield Road started living there, too, as owner-occupiers.

However, as Montpelier became more absorbed into the inner city, the street gradually became more run down. Residents of our house were now likely to be working class traders or skilled artisans. After the Second World War, the middle classes were moving to the newer and more spacious suburbs, leaving housing in areas closer to the city centre, like Montpelier, to lose value. In the 1960s and 70s, many of the houses were in multiple occupation, divided into flats or bedsitters.

Since the 1980s, Fairfield Road has returned to prosperity. It now has less crime and more young families moving in. But it also suffers from more graffiti and inflated house prices. Its residents work in a range of sectors, reflecting

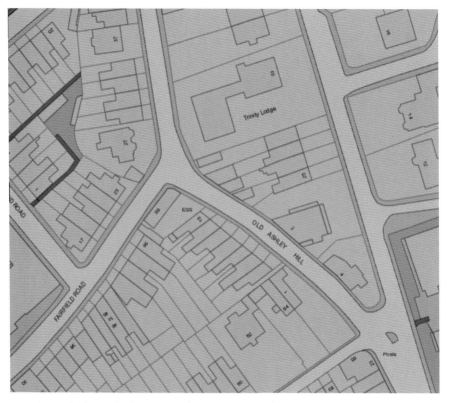

2017 Street Plan from Bristol Know Your Place website. 60 Fairfield Road is at last clearly marked as an address, on the corner at the top of Old Ashley Hill.

Bristol's very broad employment base.

Montpelier is now known as a bohemian and artistic community. One survey, in 2018, labelled it the UK's "hippest" neighbourhood. This was because of its independent cafes and shops, and its cosmopolitan, ethnically diverse, population of students, artists, designers and other creative people.[74]

Researching and writing this book has been a steep learning curve for us, albeit a very enjoyable one. Just because you own or rent a house doesn't suddenly make you an expert on its history and past residents. However, it's amazing what you can pick up very quickly if you put your mind to it, and with a little help from friends.

Our deeds are unusually complete for an old house, and we were already drawn to the exotic-sounding names in them, like the Bearpackers, Shurmer Bath and Jacob Crook. From that starting point, online newspaper archives

Fairfield Road at its junction with Falkland Road in September 2019, with number 60 in the background

and various family ancestry websites also provided invaluable sources for our research. The same websites enabled access to the Quaker records, which are especially detailed. We then studied original documents and trade directories kept in Bristol Archives or the Central Reference Library.

Inevitably, there have been a few red herrings in the process. It would be astounding if there are no mistakes in this book, although we've done our very best to eliminate them. I know we narrowly escaped a couple of howlers. House history detective work is time-consuming, quite addictive and can drive your family mad. But it's the most fun I've ever had on a laptop. We hope our experience will encourage many other people to delve into the secrets of their own house through time.

ACKNOWLEDGEMENTS

My thanks go, first and foremost, to my wife, Sue Cullimore, who made me see the wood for the trees and was the first to realise my retirement hobby could be turned into a book. She has provided all its academic rigour. Sue also came up with all the best ideas for its structure, did some of the research and wrote the tips on house history research.

Then to the production team from *A House Through Time*. By shortlisting 60 Fairfield Road for their Bristol series, they inspired us to become house history detectives ourselves. Without that initial push, our book would never have been written.

I also owe my friend and ex-neighbour Roger Ford. He literally put Spring Cottage on the map with his technical expertise at Know Your Place, knowledge of local history and eye for minute detail, which prevented quite a few errors.

My chief history buddy, Linda Taylor, is a retired college librarian, who showed me the ropes in the reference section at Bristol Central Library. She was always first on my list for advice and approval at every stage of the writing.

Mary Wright, the doyenne of history authors in Bristol, introduced me to the exotically named people associated with our house, such as the Bearpackers, Shurmer Bath and Jacob Crook. Her books on Montpelier and research notes on our deeds have been a constant port of call for fact-checking.

Paul Bullivant is a local professional photographer who offered his services for free. He took nearly all the interior photos of 60 Fairfield Road and its garden, as well as others around the city. He added the visual quality that had been missing. His skill, generosity and enthusiasm are much appreciated.

Allie Dillon, City Archivist, checked over the sections on how to use Bristol Archives and other resources to find out about the history of your own house. She also flagged up *The Diary of Sarah Fox* as a source, which proved to be a treasure trove. Thanks to her also for facilitating our use of Archives and Museums services and images from their collections.

Clive Burlton, of Bristol Books, stopped us giving up hope with publishers, while his colleague Joe Burt worked his magic on the design.

Professor Steve Poole, head of UWE's Regional History Centre, gave us crucial feedback on a draft of the book, so that we adjusted its focus to combine what we discovered with how to do something similar yourself.

I'm also grateful to his colleague, Dr Jonathan Harlow, for making me think of a better title than the "tired cliché" used originally. It was a classic example of being cruel to be kind.

Their fellow History academic, Dr Madge Dresser, retrieved from obscurity *The Diary of Sarah Fox*, and so provided intimate details about the first builder and tenant of Spring Cottage, Shurmer Bath, that were pure gold. Her publications on slavery, Bristol Quakers and working women of the eighteenth century were invaluable sources, too.

I am indebted to another local author, Shirley Hodgson, who wrote *Bristol's Pauper Children*. She took the trouble to put me right following my identity mix-up between the child servant Ada Tovey's younger brother and a second boy of the same name.

Penny Gane, our star past resident of the twentieth century, came round for coffee. It was her first return visit to 60 Fairfield Road since moving out in 1984. She offered us personal memories of her time in the house and what it meant to her.

The organisers of the *Bauhaus in Bristol* exhibition, which featured designs commissioned by Penny's grandfather in the 1930s, were very helpful with information and in allowing us to photograph the exhibits.

Thanks also to descendants of Stoker Petty Officer Ern Fiddes, especially his great niece, Sue Harris. She told us about names and family connections and supplied all the photos on page 106.

All the newspaper images reproduced in this book have been authorised for our use by the British Newspaper Archive, on behalf of the British Library, which owns the copyright. Eddie Bundy, data and copyright executive for the BNA, also gave me warm encouragement about the book and valuable tips on downloading material from their archive for publication.

All post-1800 maps reproduced in this book were downloaded from the Know Your Place website. Their use was authorised by Bristol Archives, which owns the copyright.

Finally, thanks also to our multi-talented son Tom. His artworks, from when he was a student at Bristol School of Art, feature prominently in many photos of rooms in our house.

BIBLIOGRAPHY

Books

Anscomb, Charles, *Submariner*, William Kimber & Co, 1957

Bolton, David, *Made in Bristol: 50 Stories of Local Enterprise and Invention*, Redcliffe Press, 2011

Dresser, Madge, *Slavery Obscured: The Social History of the Slave Trade in Bristol*, Redcliffe Press, 2007

Dresser, Madge (editor): *The Diary of Sarah Fox nee Champion 1745-1802*, Bristol Record Society, 2003

Dresser, Madge, *Middling Women and Work in Eighteenth Century Bristol*, UWE Bristol Research Repository, 2019

Fraser, Antonia, *Perilous Question: The Drama of the Great Reform Bill 1832*, Weidenfeld & Nicolson, 2013

Harvey, Charles; Press, Jon (editors), *Studies in the Business History of Bristol*, Bristol Academic Press, 1988

Hodgson, Shirley, *Bristol's Pauper Children*, Bristol Books, 2017

Holmes, Richard, *The Age of Wonder*, Harper Press, 2008

Kent, Oliver; Witt, Cleo; Yeo, Chris: *The Bauhaus in Bristol*, Stephen Morris, 2019

Latimer, John, *The Annals of Bristol in the Eighteenth Century*, Bristol, 1893

Leech, Roger, *The Town House in Medieval and Early Modern Bristol*, English Heritage, 2014

Moon, Robert Charles, *The Morris Family of Philadelphia Descendants of Anthony Morris 1654-1721, vol. 4*, Philadelphia, 1908

Rees, Charlotte, *Sermons*, Bristol,1796 (Google Books)

Schiffer, Michael Brian, *Draw the Lightning Down – Benjamin Franklin and Electrical Technology in the Age of Enlightenment*, University of California Press, 2003

Wright, Mary, *Montpelier - a Bristol Suburb*, Phillimore & Co, 2004

Wright, Mary, *The Blue Maids Orphanage*, Avon Local History & Archaeology, 2009

Websites

Ancestry: https://www.ancestry.co.uk/

Birmingham Workhouse: http://www.workhouses.org.uk/Birmingham/

Birmingham Workhouse (photo attribution): https://creativecommons.org/licenses/by-sa/3.0/deed.en

Bristol Poll Book 1835: https://www.ancestry.co.uk/search/collections/2410/

British Newspaper Archive: https://www.britishnewspaperarchive.co.uk/
Bath Chronicle & Weekly Gazette
Biggleswade Chronicle
Bristol Magpie
Bristol Mercury
Bristol Times & Mirror
Leeds Mercury
London Gazette
Morning Post
Monmouthshire Merlin
Perry's Bankruptcy Gazette
South Wales Daily News
Western Daily Press

Database of Classical Scholars, Rutgers University: https://dbcs.rutgers.edu/

Find A Grave: https://www.findagrave.com/

Find My Past: https://www.findmypast.co.uk/

HMS Tempest crew: http://www.hansonclan.co.uk/Royal%20Navy/tempest_crew.htm

Know Your Place: https://www.bristol.gov.uk/planning-and-building-regulations/know-your-place

The Morris Family of Philadelphia https://archive.org/details/morrisfamilyphioounkngoog/page/n165

Newport, a Brief History of: http://www.localhistories.org/Newport.html

University of Edinburgh Centre for Global History: *English Emigration to Canada 1900-1914* https://www.ed.ac.uk/history-classics-archaeology/centre-global-history/projects/english-canada

York University (Toronto), Department of History: *Salvation Army Immigrant Women and Children 1900-1930*: https://hssh.journals.yorku.ca

Trade Directories (kept in Bristol Central Library)

Hunt & Co's Directory of Bristol & Gloucester, 1849 and 1850

Kelly's Directory of Bristol, 1889 and 1922 to 1926

Mathews' Annual Bristol Directories, 1793 to 1872

Pigot's Directory of Gloucestershire, 1830

Post Office Directory of Gloucestershire, Bath and Bristol, 1856 and 1863

Sketchley's Bristol Directory of 1775

Wright's Annual Bristol Directories 1873 to 1920

Other

Bristol Archives, Ref 4964: Lands at Ashley

Bristol Archives, Ref. 6378/34: legal settlement between Shurmer Bath's heirs and Bearpacker sisters, 1809

Bristol Archives, Ref. SF/A10/1A: Friend's School at Quakers Friars, committee minutes from 1790

Bristol Museums and Galleries Collections

Bristol Poll Book, 1835

Land Registry, Gloucester

Title Deeds of Spring Cottage/60 Fairfield Road

University of Bristol Special Collections

ENDNOTES

Chapter 1: Eighteenth Century

1   Wright, Mary, *Montpelier – a Bristol Suburb*, 2004, p. 48
2   Lands at Ashley, Bristol Archives, 4964
3   Conveyance Bath/Bearpacker, Bristol Archives, 6378/34
4   London Apprenticeship Abstracts 1442-1850
5   The Monthly Magazine, September 1800, p. 198
6   Rees, Charlotte, preface by Shurmer Bath to *Sermons*, 1796
7   Moon, Robert Charles, *The Morris Family of Philadelphia Descendants of Anthony Morris 1654-1721, vol. 4,* 1908, pp. 109-116
8   Various authors, *Studies in the Business History of Bristol,* 1988, pp. 46-49
9   *The Morris Family of Philadelphia* archive, pp. 111-112
10   Dresser, Madge, *Slavery Obscured,* 2007, pp. 131-132
11   *The Diary of Sarah Fox née Champion 1745-1802,* edited by Madge Dresser, 2003
12   Ditto, p. 8
13   Ditto, p. 77
14   Schiffer, Michael Brian, *Benjamin Franklin and Electrical Technology in the Age of Enlightenment,* 2003, pp. 135-143
15   Holmes, Richard, *The Age of Wonder,* 2008, pp. 273-274, pp. 285-286, pp. 295-299
16   *The Diary of Sarah Fox,* pp. 111
17   Ditto, p. 120
18   Dresser, Madge, *Middling Women and Work in Eighteenth Century Bristol,* 2019, pp.21-22
19   Friends School Friars, including pamphlet *Rules of Friends School Bristol,* Bristol Archives, SF/A10/1A
20   Mathews' Bristol Directory, 1815
21   Bristol Museums and Galleries Collections (online narrative about Blind School)
22   *The Diary of Sarah Fox,* p. 135
23   Ditto, p. 182
24   Ditto, p. 205
25   Ditto, p. 217
26   Ditto, p. 219

Chapter 2: Early Nineteenth Century

27   Latimer, *The Annals of Bristol in the Eighteenth Century,* pp. 494-495
28   Wright, Mary, *Montpelier – a Bristol Suburb,* 2004, p. 48
29   Deeds of Spring Cottage/60 Fairfield Road (Abstract of Title, 1898)
30   Bristol Archives, Jacob Crook's will from Index of Wills proved in Bristol, 42203
31   Research notes by Mary Wright for owners on deeds of Spring Cottage/60 Fairfield Road and other documents
32   Mary Wright's research notes

Chapter 3: Mid Nineteenth Century

33   Gloucestershire Land Tax Records 1713-1833, Gloucestershire Archives
34   Wright, Mary, *The Blue Maids Orphanage,* 2009, pp. 13-14
35   *Studies in the Business History of Bristol,* 1988, pp. 56-57
36   Mathews' Bristol Directory, 1836
37   Deeds of Spring Cottage/60 Fairfield Road; Land Tax Records; Mathews' Bristol Directories
38   Wright, Mary, *The Blue Maids Orphanage,* 2009, pp. 8-11
39   Lambert, Tim, *A Brief History of Newport*
40   Mathews' Bristol Directory, 1826; Pigot's Directory of Gloucestershire, 1830

41   Leech, Roger, *The Town House in Medieval and Early Modern Bristol,* 2014, p.47
42   Dresser, Madge, Introduction to *The Diary of Sarah Fox,* p. xiv
43   Database of Classical Scholars, Rutgers University
44   Ancestry website, family tree section, *Mystery of Guillaume, Montmorency and De Beaumont,* posted 2011
45   Pigot's Directory of Gloucestershire 1830
46   Fraser, Antonia, *Perilous Question: The Drama of the Great Reform Bill,* 2013, pp. 167-170
47   Perry's Bankruptcy Gazette, 18 July 1846 and 29 May 1852
48   Certified copy of death certificate from General Register Office
49   *The Workhouse: story of an institution,* website created by Peter Higginbotham in 2000

Chapter 4: Late Nineteenth Century

50   Deeds of Spring Cottage/60 Fairfield Road
51   Wright's Bristol Directories, 1893 and 1894
52   Bolton, David, *Made in Bristol,* 2011, p. 13
53   Deeds of Spring Cottage/60 Fairfield Road

Chapter 5: First Half of Twentieth Century

54   Deeds of Spring Cottage/60 Fairfield Road; Land Registry, Gloucester
55   Wright, Mary, *Montpelier – a Bristol Suburb,* 2004, pp. 76-78
56   Ditto, pp. 79-80
57   UK Outward Passenger Lists and Canadian Passenger Lists, via Ancestry website
58   British Columbia Death Index, 1872-1990, via Ancestry website
59   *English Emigration to Canada 1900-1914,* research paper, University of Edinburgh Centre for Global History, 2014
60   Hodgson, Shirley, *Bristol's Pauper Children,* 2017
61   Rutherdale, Myra, *Salvation Army Immigrant Women and Children 1900-1930,* research paper, York University (Toronto), 2007
62   Wright, Mary, *Montpelier – a Bristol Suburb,* 2004, p. 75
63   Mary Wright's research notes on deeds of Spring Cottage/Fairfield Road
64   Bolton, David, *Made in Bristol,* 2011, pp. 1-2
65   Deeds of Spring Cottage/60 Fairfield Road
66   Wright's Directory 1895, Kelly's Directories 1922-1926
67   UK, Commonwealth War Graves 1939-1947, for Ernest Herbert Alfred Fiddes, via Ancestry website
68   Hansonclan website, recording the Royal Navy service history of a survivor from the *HMS Tempest* sinking
69   Anscomb, Charles, *Submariner,* 1957
70   Electoral Registers

Chapter 6: Up to the Present Day

71   Information from Penny Gane
72   Kent, Oliver, *The Bauhaus in Bristol,* 2019
73   Information from Penny Gane
74   *Evening Standard,* 2 Feb 2018 (Travelsupermarket.com 'Hip-hangout Neighbourhood Index', 2018)